Vet behind the ears

Christopher Timothy

Vet behind the ears

Pan Original Pan Books London and Sydney

First published 1979 by Pan Books Ltd,
Cavaye Place, London SW10 9PG
© Christopher Timothy 1979
ISBN 0 330 26075 8
Printed and bound in Great Britain by
Richard Clay (The Chaucer Press) Ltd, Bungay, Suffolk

to Simon, Nicholas, Robin, Tabitha, Kate and
David and everyone to whom I owe so much –
they know who they are

Very special thanks to Nigel Crewe without
whose help this book very simply would not
have been written

'Never act with children or animals.' So said W. C. Fields.
As I sit here surrounded by six kids and looking through the
scripts of *All Creatures Great and Small* I can't help wondering
what I would like to have said to the great Hollywood comic.

I'm sure he would have disapproved of my close relationship
with cows. He would have had a strong word to say about my
involvement with horses. Dogs, cats and rabbits would have
flummoxed him; Tricki Woo would have left him speechless.
But then, what is the terrible secret behind Tricki Woo? Indeed,
is there a secret behind Tricki Woo?

Mrs Pumphrey had sent a Fortnum and Mason hamper as a
thank-you to James Herriot. It contained three bottles of
excellent brandy. In the studio the production assistant
carefully pointed out to me that two of the bottles were the real
thing and cost about £80 apiece. The third wasn't, and so it was
the one we were to open. I had to be absolutely certain that when
I passed a bottle to Tristan it was this one.

The camera started to roll.

'Open this, will you Tristan?' I said to Peter Davison as I
passed him a bottle.

'This one?' queried Tristan looking a bit surprised.

'Yes,' I said.

'Are you certain?' Tristan asked very doubtfully.

What on earth was wrong with Peter Davison? He had always
stuck to the script before; what's more, it was very unlike
Tristan to have second thoughts about opening any bottle.

'Yes. Open it!' I said, exasperated.

The camera carried on filming. If this was a concoction made
by the props department, I thought as I sipped from the glass
Tristan handed me, then they were very clever. I had expected

water, coloured with tea leaves, which would only *look* like brandy.

'Cut,' called the director.

'For goodness sake! What have you done?' exclaimed the production assistant as he rushed back on to the set. Of course, in the heat of the moment, it was the wrong bottle I had passed to Peter Davison. No wonder he had suddenly acted out of character. It was delicious.

But did we deserve it?

The *Radio Times* has been full of letters that ask, 'Why, oh why, must we see Christopher Timothy going up a cow's rear quarters again and again? Don't vets do anything else?' Some simply state, 'Of course, Christopher Timothy doesn't really do it. It's a trick with the camera. It's a real vet whose arms we see.'

The camera is very good at creating illusions, but what is the point at which the camera stops and real life takes over?

At the end of every interview I am always asked if there are some funny stories I could tell. Well, there are. I hope they are not confusing.

When, as teenagers, my brother Jon and I were in the kitchen with our grandmother, Jon asked her where the tea was. 'It's in the tin marked biscuits,' she said. Taking down the tin and looking into it, he pronounced ,'No. This is coffee.' To which Gran inexplicably replied, 'Ah yes! But that's *real* coffee.'

It is this kind of zany logic that runs in the family. You are warned!

chapter one

'I'm only interested in playing James Herriot,' I heard myself say with the appalling clarity of someone else's speech. This time I had well well and truly 'blown it', I thought as I watched the producer opposite me aghast; my face froze and my eyes glazed in horror at my precipitous words.

Well, it wouldn't be the first time that an over-hasty word had jettisoned me unexpectedly into the deep end of a pool I was only inspecting from the edge. Some thirty-seven years of fairly relentless activity had necessitated some hard swimming.

'Ho-hum,' I muttered to myself, 'here we go again.' I turned to look out of the window on to the grey, uninspiring walls of the Television Centre's inner court.

Being in the theatre, I reflected, is really like being at a sort of perpetual crossroads. The trick is to go along the right road at the right time. Some roads are dead-end, others potter along aimlessly, yet others lead all the way to El Dorado. (Of course, El Dorado does depend rather on the kind of fulfilment you are after.) They all criss-cross each other endlessly. Perhaps only in hindsight can you see the route you should have taken. All you can say is: this is the route that presents itself – and go for it.

The television series *All Creatures Great and Small*, from the moment I had heard there might be a possibility of being in it, I had certainly gone for.

I was already working at the BBC on the comedy series *Murder Most English*, playing Anton Rodgers' side-kick, Sid. One day as we sat in the canteen at the recording studios in Birmingham, aimlessly stirring what seemed to be our millionth cup of tea of the day, by way of conversation I asked the producer what he would be doing when *Murder* was all over.

'We are trying to get the rights to those James Herriot books,' he said. 'We'd like to make a series of them.'

'Well, it's a foregone conclusion,' I said, summarily deciding against another lump of sugar. 'It'll be a hit.'

'That's if we get the rights,' he said, with a vague chuckle, before mentally re-ascending to those Olympian heights of decision-making occupied only by politicians and television producers.

'Yes,' I replied – more a sort of convivial grunt really. I would have that lump of sugar after all, I thought, and I sploshed it into my tea.

Well, still another three episodes to go on *Murder Most English*, another month of hard work, great fun and total involvement. Probably the most enjoyable job I had done to date, I reflected. Horrible to think it would come to an end. And then what? Something good was going to happen, I knew. It was in the air, I thought. Somehow the struggle and grind of survival was going to give me a break, I just knew it was. A momentary surge of optimism spun rivulets of tea into my saucer. In a month, I thought, anything can happen.

The days rushed by as days only do when they are crammed full of enjoyable activity. Not until we neared the last few days of *Murder Most English* did I hear any more about *All Creatures Great and Small*.

The completion of any film-work assumes the atmosphere of the end of term at school. 'And what are you going to do in the holidays, Timothy?' requires only a slight twist to make it 'And what are you doing next?' which is bandied about the set. The production team all know; they are on to the next project. Only a very few of the actors actually have jobs lined up. Usually, though, the reply is, 'I'm not certain at the moment . . . There are a few things in the air.' This means, 'I haven't got a clue, but as I have some money in my pocket and I don't finish working until ten o'clock tonight I'm not panicking yet.' But agitating your agent has started some days before, and suddenly you realize you have been keeping your ear unusually close to the ground, and planning the next batch of letters you are to write. There are not going to be any holidays.

As we stood about on the set one day, by now well into the time when you have to restrain yourself from making minute-by-minute calls to your agent to see what is happening with your career, someone said something very foolish.

'I have a feeling you're in line for James Herriot,' this someone muttered and then looked blank as if they had said nothing at all.

To say a thing like that to an actor who faces imminent unemployment is not dissimilar to lighting a short fuse to a very big bomb.

'Sorry? What was that?' I said. But whoever it was who had said that had gone. A voice from the 'gods' had called, 'OK. Ready to go again,' and the knot of people had evaporated into thin air, leaving me rooted to the floor.

'Chris, can you hit your marks please. We're ready to go,' said a scurrying floor assistant.

'Yes,' I murmured, and wandered back to my position stunned as if half a dozen arc lamps had fallen one after the other on to my head. The part of James Herriot had never even occurred to me. After that brief word with Bill Sellars in the canteen a few weeks before, I had not given it another thought.

'Apparently I'm being considered for the lead in the James Herriot series. You know, the vet books they're going to do,' I said with the utmost casualness I could muster to Brenda Bruce, who was also in *Murder Most English*.

'Well, good luck dear,' she replied. 'I'm sure you're very right for it.'

'Am I?' I said. 'I don't know. I'd better read the books, then.'

The half-hour until tea-break seemed an eternity. There were only two requests that I should concentrate on what I was doing.

'Sue! Sue!' I gushed down the telephone to my ever patient wife when finally the tea-break came. 'When you pick up the kids from school can you whip into the bookshop and get all the Herriot books? They're in paperback.'

'Yes, but why?' she asked.

'Tell you later. Can't stop. See you this evening.' Next call to my agents.

'Any news?' I bleated.

'No. Nothing since you called at lunchtime,' came the reply, with only the slightest trace of sarcasm.

'I'm just calling on the off-chance,' I said, always hopeful.

'Yes, of course.' It would have been hard to say it any more noncommittally.

'You see, I've just heard something on the grapevine and I wondered if anything official had come through.'

'As soon as we hear anything we'll let you know.'

At last, weeks later, there I was sitting opposite the producer. Could I really be saying, 'I'm only interested in playing James Herriot'? After all, my priority had always been to stay in work. All the producer, Bill Sellars, had asked was would I be interested in playing Tristan?

It's all or nothing, I thought, jeopardizing at a stroke the lives of my wife and six kids, not to mention the mortgage.

Strange now to think I could say that. The part of Tristan, lacking only the name, was equally important. In the event, Peter Davison who plays him – and a very good mate of mine he is too – is so absolutely right it is difficult to envisage anyone else in the part.

'I would really rather play James Herriot,' I reiterated limply, shuffling in my chair.

'Well . . . In all honesty I'm under pressure to get an established star,' said the producer.

When someone says they are telling you something 'in all honesty' you know you are about to hear something horrible. It sounds dreadfully familiar, I thought, but just said, 'I see,' as neutrally as possible whilst the dead-end signs shot up immutably before my eyes.

The useful thing about an actor's training is that, whilst truly world-shattering events go on around or even inside him, he can maintain an absolutely impassive face; perhaps even manage a smile like the ballet dancer does as her body is twisted into pain-racked knots – outwardly seeming to produce a graceful effect.

'But I've heard this so many times before!' I wanted to shout. 'It makes me sick! How am I ever going to be a star name if I'm

12

never given a star part? Make me a star! The series is strong enough to carry someone who isn't a name if he is right for the part. And I am right . . . I am right, I tell you!'

But of course I didn't say this, nor even show it in my face. Impassively I just said again, 'Yes . . . I see,' and probably glowed a little red.

'So there you have it. Trust me and we'll see what we can do.'

'Yes.'

'Won't be long now. We'll let you know what we've decided shortly. Nice to see you again.'

'Goodbye, and thanks for seeing me.'

'Goodbye.'

I've blown it! I've blown it, I thought. But how could I have? I was really in with a chance! Walking through the winding corridors on my way out, it was difficult to behave like a normal person. The adrenalin pumping through me combined with the necessary quiet restraint of the last twenty-five minutes made me want to shout, scream and gibber like an idiot. Those corridors at the Television Centre must have seen some strange sights in their time. Building maintenance staff would do well to take out an added insurance policy for the place; only a football special can have to carry such potential combustion as do those interminable passages at the BBC.

Gradually I began to calm down. I was just in the usual post-interview state. How an actor manages to remain youthful-looking and carefree, not go bald and wrinkled years ahead of time, this must be one of the wonders of the world.

Down, down I went into the deepest depression. 'But the indications were so good,' I groaned as I kicked open the exit door and felt the familiar grey drizzle settle on my face.

All around me on the Underground from White City into town sat fellow travellers quietly reading their newspapers or placidly smoking a cigarette and staring blankly in the direction of the window, blissfully unaware of the turmoil that bubbled and boiled so near to them.

The interview was done for good or bad. All I had to do was

13

wait. What did it matter anyway? So on with the grind. I must phone my agent. He was saying someone was interested in me for something else. I wasn't going to hang about.

People in other careers go through the interview process perhaps only once every few years. As an actor you can do it half a dozen times in a week. It is something you never really get used to. Of course you develop an interview technique, but even the gentlest person has to grow a thick skin to take the almost inevitable rejections that come one on top of the other in this very overcrowded profession. You 'lay yourself on the line', wishing to present yourself in the truest and therefore probably most vulnerable light. You more than likely convince yourself you are the right person for the part. However kindly the rejection is worded, it is still *no*, and feels like a punch in the stomach. It is hard to be impervious for long. Naturally there are times when, for various reasons, getting or not getting the job is not that important. If it is something big, though, chances are it could well alter the whole course of your life. The expectation is very great and therefore the rejection, if it comes, is doubly hard. Meanwhile, life goes on around you, and your frayed and battered nervous system still has to take you round the supermarket, on and off the bus, and read bedtime stories to the kids to put them to sleep.

Something you need in the theatre world is the power of quick recovery, I reflected as the Underground drew into Waterloo. It's a sort of roulette game – not an original perception, I realized, gathering my legs up under me and preparing for the sixty-second dash to catch the next train home. But I had just seen three years of regular income, security, and perhaps celebrity too, all disappear within the time it takes to say seven words rather fast.

'But I do only want to play James Herriot,' I almost said out loud. So great was the impetus of this thought that I must have caught the train with a good thirty seconds to spare.

The rhythmical rattling of the train down to Guildford would have at other times produced a sort of stupor in me. Tranquilliz-

14

ing as it was, the journey was almost over before it began to take effect.

I must stop thinking about the interview, I told myself, giving a kick to someone's empty cigarette packet and hurtling it across the compartment floor.

I remembered the hastily whispered phonecall from the BBC a few weeks before. Another friend had just heard Bill Sellars say, as he left the viewing theatre after watching a preview of *Murder Most English*, 'Well, it's obvious who should play Herriot,' and the implication had been that it was me he was talking about.

A call had been made to my agents to find out if I could do a Scottish accent. James Herriot was supposed to have a Scottish accent. I put two and two together . . .

And then there was the lunch, some days later in the BBC Club with some old friends, all BBC staff, people who were 'in the know', if anyone was. There had been the usual questions: 'What are you doing now, Chris?' 'What are you about to do?' to which my rather veiled reply was, 'Oh, there's something in the air.' This had been speedily squashed: 'If you mean James Herriot, forget it. You're not going to get it – ' depressing me no end because, in fact, that's exactly what I did mean.

It took the long walk to my agents' offices to lift that one. The juggling act required to keep my unemployed morale high had really received a knocking. Yet this time, I told myself, I was not wrong to hope. It was in the air: something good was about to happen; but not *All Creatures* . . . then. The BBC people would know if anybody did.

By the time I reached my agents that afternoon I was ready to chuck the whole idea. It was only a fantasy. 'Forget it. Forget the Herriot,' I said as I went in the door.

'Just shut up a moment. Don't be over hasty. Bill Sellars wants to see you tomorrow, OK?'

A lightning readjustment was called for. I had to sit down. Within moments my withered hopes revived.

15

'Wonderful,' I said, and meant it . . . The days of waiting had already begun to pass – and, with six young children in the house, life, as always, would be pretty hectic.

I love my work. From the outset I have been lucky, but if the business has given me financial return it is only because of the amount of energy I have ploughed into it.

You see the problem. Whatever happens, I must ensure there is an adequate income. I think life in the theatre easily produces a sort of passiveness. So much time is spent sitting around waiting for other people to make up their minds that after a time it is difficult to keep the initial aggressive fire going. That fire is absolutely essential. The happy result is that my time is ceaselessly taken up with working out the various permutations for successful survival, a sort of battle of wits.

Enough public self-examination! However, I do want to set the background to some of my more 'theatrical' stories. When people in this business behave in a funny way or say outrageous things, it is usually because there are fairly extreme pressures at work on a temperament that is probably already a bit unbalanced: 'artistic' and all that. It is a way of life I relish. I could not and would not change it for anything. I don't mean to make it sound like a race apart. Of course it isn't. The theatre world is just a shade nearer the public eye than most.

On my last day at drama school, as I had bounded down the front steps, finally on my way out into the big wide world, some-one had called to me, 'See you in the dole queue, Chris.' 'No, you won't!' I shouted back. Actually, I'd said something a bit stronger than that. For an actor, we had been told, the labour exchange is a fact of life. But I was determined to prove them wrong.

Having got some of these simple philosophical statements over with . . . with the plot.

I had to wait ten days before I heard anything more about *All Creatures Great and Small*. What a cruel length of time to wait that was! With no conclusive word it's difficult to dismiss any job from your mind, try as you might. You attempt to apply some sort of time factor to it as a kind of sanity guard – so crippling can the tensions be if you let them. 'If I don't hear within three days,' you mutter to yourself, 'then I haven't got it.' But at the end of those three days you can't quite let optimism die. 'If I haven't heard tomorrow then I definitely haven't got it,' you say, and so it goes on. Ten days! When I finally heard, hope was a very small thing indeed . . .

You might expect to hear something of the magnitude of getting the part of James Herriot through the official channels of your agent. 'I've just had a call from the BBC,' the rather matter-of-fact voice over the telephone might go. 'Yes, yes!' you'd want to scream, hope and fear holding you frozen in your tracks. 'We were talking about the part of James Herriot in *All Creatures Great and Small*. If you remember it was one of the things you had an interview for.' 'How could I ever forget?' you'd want to shout, such was your agitation, but you'd bite back the words, appearing instead as though you had only just now dimly remembered the fact: 'Oh yes . . . I remember now.' 'Well . . .' continues your agent, life and death seeming now to hang in the balance.

But no such luck. After fifteen years I can cope with that sort of phonecall, although it often occurs to me that that is how I'm going to die. Instead of just playing it cool as my agent does, one day I shall just go pop!

I had been doing a quick appearance in an episode of *The Saint*. As with any filming, it had been a long day and it was not until about nine o'clock in the evening that I got home.

'Simon has something to tell you,' said Sue by way of a greeting as I walked in through the kitchen door.

Simon, my oldest child, now aged about fourteen, was going through an unfortunate phase of smashing windows with his football.

'Simon!' I bellowed automatically, thinking of all the windows I had replaced. 'Your mother tells me that you've got something to tell me.' I was feeling very much the dictatorial father.

'Yeah?' he said, ambling in from where the kids had all been watching the television in the sitting-room, and slouching up against the kitchen door.

'Well?'

'You got the job. All right?'

The harsh words, barely formulated on my tongue, dribbled back into my throat.

With a cursory 'You OK, Dad?' Simon nonchalantly disappeared into the hallway.

'James Herriot! It's mine! Iv'e got it! I've got the part!' I gibbered at Sue, grabbing her and dancing a wild tattoo around the kitchen.

'It's wonderful,' she said, 'but be quiet! We haven't told Robin yet.'

Robin, our third son, must have been about eight at the time.

'When he came in from school,' she continued, 'he said, "I've been praying all day, so he will get it, won't he?" I told him it would help. So you'd better go and tell him.'

I went through to the sitting-room where Simon, Nicky, Robin and Tabitha all sat glued to *Kojak*.

'Robin,' I said, perching on the arm of the chair and trying momentarily to catch his attention. 'I've got something to tell you.'

He turned from the hypnosis of the television to look at me inquiringly, more out of politeness than interest.

'I've got the job.'

The rhythm unbroken, he turned back to *Kojak*. 'I know,' he said in a deadpan voice. 'I prayed.'

chapter two

Before doing *All Creatures Great and Small* I may have had no great experience of animals, but I certainly did know about kids. Perhaps the experiences were not all that different.

My kids are well used to an actor father, and take the ups and downs of my life with an equanimity only to be wondered at. To go home now is a great delight. The house seems to swarm with them. Not only are there a half-dozen of my own, ranging in age from mid-teens down to four, but all their friends are around there too. There appear to be hundreds – all presided over by Sue, a mother par excellence. Of course, in the summertime our house is at a premium, for we have a swimming pool. Surveying the lawn I often think the rest of Surrey must look like Hamlin did after the Pied Piper went through.

Coming home on the train one evening at a time when we had only three kids, I came across an article in the newspaper. A number of working women were expressing their views on life. All of them said how much a woman needed to go out to work, how much she must not stay at home with lots of kids, otherwise she would become a 'cabbage'. I was panic-stricken and rushed home to Sue waving the paper and thinking, 'Goodness, is this what I've done?' Sue took one look at it and said, 'What rubbish! They've done what they wanted to do; and I'm doing exactly what I want to do.'

After our fourth child, Tabitha, Sue was very strong-minded and insisted on being sterilized. 'If we want any more we can adopt,' she said. I am afraid I was not as strong-minded as she was I should have had a vasectomy. The staff nurse in the hospital deeply disapproved of the woman yet again bearing the brunt. Despite the nurse's formidable powers of persuasion, combined with her equally formidable bulk, I chickened out.

A couple of years later we did indeed adopt. First my beautiful Kate, who wants to be a dancer, and then David, who after an initially difficult time is now truly the chick of the brood.

David was eighteen months old when he came to join us. After going to visit him at his foster parents' many, many times, and letting him become thoroughly acclimatized to us, his foster mother brought him over by taxi. She was obviously feeling great emotional stress and hated to let him go. However, she rushed in, pushed a teddybear into his hands, and plonked him down with the other kids, with whom he immediately began to play. It was not until later that, wandering through to another room, David suddenly realized she had gone. Shocked, he withdrew into himself and stayed that way for several months. Later, the woman at the adoption agency, a marvellous jolly person who had been overseeing the whole project, called me into her office. She couldn't praise Sue enough for the way in which she had managed to integrate David into the family. Sue's cajolery, prompting, above all her endless patience and love, finally broke through the shell he had so completely erected about himself.

Kids are prone to imitate their parents, as we were suddenly made sharply aware one day. A very young Simon was out playing with some other children in the lane that ran in front of the house where we then lived in Essex.

'Let's be our daddies,' one of them suggested.

'Mine's a policeman,' said another, walking up and down the lane as he thought a policeman might.

'Mine works in a garage,' said a third, proceeding to mime working in a garage.

'Mine's an actor,' said Simon, and with that he threw himself to his knees, flung his arms to the sky and shouted, 'I want to be a star! I want to be a star!'

Sue and I looked at one another in astonishment. 'We've got to stop that!' we said simultaneously. It had been a joke between us, but if it got round the neighbourhood, especially in that way, we would soon be ostracized. 'Do you know how the Timothys train their children?' people would say. '. . . And we thought they seemed such a nice young couple.'

These days my kids come and visit me in the theatre or at the studios. They will always root for me, but make sure there are no 'superstars' in the home . . .

'So Dad's got this wonderful job. Great! We hoped he would, but wait until after *Kojak* is over before you get excited, or do it in another room.' That was their attitude on the evening I learned I'd got the part of James Herriot.

Sue and I skulked back into the kitchen where, with a bottle of champagne provided by the lodger, we celebrated round the kitchen table.

'Stratford Johns had to move house, you know, when he got Barlow,' was all I could think of to say.

'But we've only just got here,' said Sue.

'Better go ex-directory at least,' said the lodger; and that's about the best thing I could have done.

'Well, that's one in the eye for old Roy Newton!' I said to Sue whilst doing a sort of gargle with the champagne. It was an old joke between us. In fifteen years never a job could go by without my thinking of the kind but firm advice he'd once given me.

When I'd left the Priory Grammar School in Shrewsbury, I'd left under a cloud. My mother had constantly to remind herself of Winston Churchill's fine example. I was out in the world with one O-level and no other qualifications of any sort. Winston Churchill too had been none too successful at school and, like me, the despair of all who came into contact with him. My mother had battled to remind herself of the brilliant man he had become. After one or two minor setbacks I was put to work in one of Shrewsbury's august and well-established family businesses – FRANK NEWTON – GENTS' OUTFITTERS ran the proud legend over the shop window. It was at that time being run by Mr Frank Newton's two sons, Mr Frank and Mr Roy.

One day as I was shuffling some stock around, deep in the bowels of the shop, Mr Roy asked me what my expectations were. I don't know what prompted him to inquire. I was at the time very earnest and anxious to please. Scurrying about my work I am sure now I was beneath anybody's attention, let alone a kindly word.

'Well, I want to go to drama school and be an actor,' I blurted out.

I knew I was saying this to a man whose name was a byword the length and breadth of Shrewsbury: as an amateur actor there was not an award he had not won. The silence seemed endless. Oh goodness! What have I said? I thought as I shifted uneasily on my spindly adolescent legs. What would my long-suffering mother say if I arrived home early only to tell her I had been sacked?

'Stick to what you're doing,' pronounced Mr Roy at long last, disarranging with a pat the Elvis Presley quiff that balanced precariously on the top of my pimply head. 'Work your way up and do all the acting you want as an amateur, or you'll end up in West End bars scrounging drinks from other out-of-work actors.'

'Yes, Mr Roy. Thank you, Mr Roy.' I breathed a sigh of relief. At any rate I had not got the sack.

Those words meant so kindly to deter me and push some common-sense into my head of course had had the opposite effect, although it was not for another three years that I did finally get to drama school. Then, I seemed to be light years away...

With the champagne and the excitement, the lights twinkled from the Timothy household late into the night.

My initial reaction had been to telephone everybody I knew to tell them of the wonderful news. That evening I settled for my parents and an actor friend, Richard O'Callaghan. Together we had played in Tom Stoppard's *Rosencrantz and Guildenstern are Dead* for a seven-month run at London's Criterion Theatre. Playing Rosencrantz and Guildenstern respectively, as those who have seen the play will know, we had to have a very close working relationship, rather more so than perhaps in other plays. The two characters are on stage rabbiting away to each other for the entire duration of the play. It is a brilliant piece of theatre.

Basically, the plot is Shakespeare's *Hamlet* turned upside down. Rosencrantz and Guildenstern are the two shadowy student friends of Hamlet summoned to the Danish Court to help fathom his strange behaviour. Only fleetingly do they pass through Shakespeare's play, and nobody even has the time or concern to sort out which if them is Rosencrantz and which Guildenstern. Tom Stoppard's play follows their activities as they hang about the court waiting to be summoned, increasingly confused as to their purpose there, playing endless word games, and even becoming confused themselves as to their own identities. If people, looking at *Hamlet*, say 'Gosh! I could never learn the lines,' something that is quite a feat even for an actor trained in the art, then equally would they be daunted by *Rosencrantz and Guildenstern are Dead*. There seem to be millions of words!

All of which is to say that performing with another actor can be a strangely intimate experience. On one level you know that person deeply, whereas on the more practical day-to-day level hardly at all. Especially true in the case of Stoppard's play which is so demanding. Out in front of an audience your life is in the hands of the actor playing opposite you, and vice versa. To work well, that trust is implicit and it makes life hell if it isn't there.

Richard O'Callaghan is the most generous actor I have worked with. The seven months were a total delight. I knew when I heard I had the part of James Herriot that I could tell him without any fear of that almost unavoidable actors' emotion: whilst superficially pleased at your success, at the same time they cannot but feel envious. Made vulnerable by this sudden news, and growing expansive with the champagne, envy was the last thing I wanted to have to cope with.

Whilst working at the National Theatre a number of years before there had been an actor in the company who was later to be in *All Creatures Great and Small*. He had owned a garage in Wales. With a wife and young family he was all set for a quiet and secure life far removed from the razzle-dazzle insecurity of the theatre. Suddenly, much to everybody's great surprise, he sold up and went to the Royal Academy of Dramatic Art in London.

Luckily he was successful and went straight from there to the National Theatre, where he played good roles. Talking to him one day, probably at a despairing moment, I had asked whatever had possessed him.

'Well, it's to do with having the spotlight on you. There are times when the spotlight is on you and times when it isn't. When it isn't you shut up, keep quiet and pay attention. When it is you take your moment.'

With *All Creatures Great and Small* I was definitely going to 'take my moment'. At the National we were told, 'You get on stage and suddenly your feet grow into it. That's your moment.'

There are also those terrible stories with which, in the spate of tell-all biographies from Hollywood, we must by now be all too familiar, and which as a young actor were seared into my brain. Tales of young actors who, in their endeavour to get to the top, might be a little too good in a scene for their own well-being, posing a threat to the star who was firmly determined to stay in the number-one position. The struggling young actor would soon discover to his detriment, despite the moment apparently being his, just whose moment it really was, and just how determined that star was to remain a star. In a Jeanette Macdonald picture nobody danced or sang better than she did, I was told, and it had got nothing to do with talent.

Robert Hardy, Siegfried in *All Creatures*, a very accomplished actor as anyone will know who has seen him both in *All Creatures* and as Albert in *Edward VII* as well as in his many other television portrayals, is wonderful at handing over these 'moments'. He always allows you to take the scene giving you centre-stage, when an actor of his distinction and experience could easily carry on regardless.

When I told my parents of my good fortune in getting the part of James Herriot they naturally were delighted. I had to make two separate phonecalls: my parents had divorced when I was seven. My mother, to escape from the Blitz, had taken myself and my younger brother Peter down to her parents' house in

Wales. My father was called to serve as an army chaplain away from home. During this time of separation they grew apart, and at the end of the war my father never came home. Finally, in 1947, they were divorced.

My brother Peter was ten months old when he died. I was three. Of the actual events I do not remember much. I was told later that I went into a state of complete shock and so I must have blacked most of it from my mind. I do remember, though, climbing on to a stool to look from the porch window on to the pram where Peter slept in the cool of the afternoon shade and seeing it was overturned. I called my mother. I remember him lying on my mother's lap as she cradled him closely. In my mind I see him covered with specks of blood, but I am told there was no blood, only perhaps a small trickle from his nose and the corner of his mouth.

About a year later my parents adopted. My brother Jon came from a home in London's Holland Park. At that time children's homes proliferated, filled with war orphans. Jon was the same age as Peter would have been.

Going with my parents to the home, whilst they stood talking with the nurse, I heard a coughing sound from behind a screen. I pushed it to one side. There lay a child tinier than I who stretched up his arms towards me.

'Look! He likes me!' I called excitedly. 'We'll have him. Can we take him now?' Of course we could not. But that was my first introduction to the smashing bloke who is my brother Jon . . .

The following morning I awoke with a start. Something good had happened the night before. It was a moment before I remembered. Ah yes . . . James Herriot. The realization flooded through me with a warm sensation in the same way the champagne had the previous night. Normally I barely drink, taking only the occasional glass of wine. Full of well-being and ready to spring from my bed, the throb in my head and the dryness of my throat brought me up sharp.

'Oh goodness! I must call my agent,' I said to Sue as she came into the room having by that time been up for hours, having

25

given the kids their breakfast and packed them off to school.

'I haven't heard officially yet. I hope it hasn't all been a sort of dream.' Having drunk most of the champagne myself the previous night I wasn't in the mood to take anything for granted.

When you are fairly positive you have got the job, it is important, and theatre lore dictates it, not to bank on it until you have the contract in your hand. With big projects, especially in the case of films, things have an unfortunate habit of not working out, or just evaporating into thin air. In fact, not until you are on the set, the lights are up, and someone calls 'Action' should you let yourself finally believe it. Every actor is full of stories of 'the one that got away'. Combining with the hangover, the thought of such a possibility added to the pounding in my head.

Worrying lest I had made the most awful fool of myself, I made a passable scamper down to the telephone.

'It's all right. You've got it.' They seemed to have second sight in that office. Maybe something of my agitation transmitted itself through the receiver.

'. . . And will you call Bill Sellars to have a talk with him,' they added, having reassured me the part was indeed mine. 'You're obviously not in a fit state to discuss details, so if you would call us back later in the day we'll tell you of the deal we've worked out. Just remember, you start in six weeks.'

As if I wouldn't call them incessantly on the slightest pretext anyway.

Bill Sellars told me that for at least a week I would be sent off to watch a real vet at work, and to get some of the feel of James Herriot's life in Yorkshire. We would then go straight into the first block of location work. This 'pre-filming' would last for six weeks, during which time the various directors involved in the twelve episodes would come up to Yorkshire and do all the external filming necessary to slot into the studio recording. All the studio work, six days' rehearsal and two days' recording for each episode, would be done on video-tape. After rehearsals in London followed by studio work in Birmingham, any further footage that was needed would be supplied by location filming for the odd day here and there. This they call 'strike filming'.

I never dared to tell Bill Sellars, and certainly only now set it down with some trepidation, my only comment being it is a strange way that life falls out, but a year or so previously I had taken a couple of my kids into the local town to see *The Towering Inferno*. Like most big cinemas it had been turned into three smaller ones. Playing alongside the film we wanted to see was one of the Herriot films staring Simon Ward. The queue for *The Towering Inferno* was very long and there was some doubt as to whether we would get in. 'Never mind, Dad,' Simon had said, 'if we can't get into this we can always go and see the vet one.' No we can't, I'd replied. 'If you want to see that you can get your mother to take you.' We did manage to get into *The Towering Inferno*.

I also asked Bill if I could tell some of my friends in the press. I was thinking particularly of the *Sun*, with whom I had had a working relationship for a number of years. His advice was not to call them, that there was a big publicity department at the BBC and to leave it to them. In the event the *Sun* provided some strange twists to the tale.

As lots of people know, every week for the last eight years I have been doing the television commercials for the *Sun*. For the last couple of years I have only been doing them as a 'voice-over'. My face does not appear. There was a time five years ago when I was doing a TV play that people said would make me into a big name. I called the *Sun* instantly and asked them if from then on I could be only the voice. I was worrying, as other actors do, that my face would become too popularly linked with just the one character, that I would be known for ever as 'the *Sun* man' and lose out on other jobs because of it. The play never came to anything and a year later I had to ask the *Sun* if I could be the 'in-vision' presenter again, as I needed the money. They were always very good to me. The whole production team soon became friends of mine, and I would look forward to the few hours spent in the studio each week.

At the time when I started to do the *Sun* commercials, this was not really the 'done thing' for an actor. Mates of mine would say 'Yes, of course you do them well, but . . .' and then nudge me, implying I should not be doing them at all. It was only with the lack of jobs and the realization that commercials made you good money that actors, well-known faces some of them, began to appear. Now virtually everyone will do them, if they get the chance, and be glad of it.

There was another problem with the *Sun*. The commercials broke new ground. Their flat one-shot format was more American hard-sell, in direct contrast to the glossy, expensive-looking commercials we were used to. With this new style, the in-vision presenter just talked into the camera very fast for sixty seconds, made the appropriate gestures for the subject matter, rapidly picked up and put down relevant 'props', and had nubile page-three girls floating around him.

'There's an interview for a commercial you might like to go to if you're interested,' my agent had said in a desultory way one day.

In the room where we all sat waiting to be summoned for the interview it struck me that there were very few actors attending. Mostly the hopefuls seemed to be sports commentators or television announcers. Eventually it was my turn to go into the interview room and parade before the assembled ranks of the production team and various interested parties; I should say 'uninterested' – such has been the experience of most inter-viewees at similar casting sessions.

You walk nervously into a room full of people all sitting about bored out of their minds. 'Oh God! Another one,' they are thinking. Scratching nit-picking, they look anywhere but at you. Momentarily you are at a loss which one to direct your attention towards. Unable to decide, you give them all a polished-tooth grin. 'And what have you done before?' one of them perks up enough energy to ask. A mere formality. As if it mattered. They don't really want to know. When you have finished relating your career to date you are left with an awful sensation that your whole life has been one big mistake. At such times I think of Athene Seyler, one of the greatest comic actresses of her day, who was being interviewed by a nervous young director. When asked what she had been doing recently she replied, 'Well, this morning I did a little shopping.'

'So what we want you to do is talk to us for sixty seconds. You read it all off these idiot-boards and these are the props. Now remember . . . you are a presenter. Sell it to us. Go!'

Silence, except for a stifled yawn from someone in a corner.

'But I can't read a thing without my glasses,' I said, 'and I haven't brought them with me.'

They all looked at each other as though they really had got a right one here. Their off-hand treatment of me made me violently angry.

'Give me the script!' I said, 'I'll be back!' Snatching the script from the desk I raced upstairs, locked myself in the lavatory and learnt hard. Ten minutes later I pushed back into the office, stood in front of them, said, 'Right, now you can have it,' took a deep breath and rattled off the sixty seconds of patter at them...

'Thank you very much for your trouble,' I said and smartly left the room. Within twenty-four hours I was told that I'd got the job.

In the event all the people connected with it turned out to be ace. When I later came to do *All Creatures Great and Small* I still continued to do the advertisements in voice only. If I had to be at rehearsals at ten o'clock I would nip in and record the commercial at nine o'clock. If I was away filming they would arrange for me to go into the recording studio nearest to me and it would be sent down to them. They were always helpful and generous in every way. I say 'were', in fact I mean 'are', for I continue to do them.

Sometimes when the *Sun* was doing an article on *All Creatures* I would find some of the patter I had to deliver would be about myself. That was very strange. 'Christopher Timothy', I would say, lowering my voice. Through the tannoy would come the message to speak up. Sometimes there would be a bit about Robert Hardy, and I would be asked, 'Could you curb your enthusiasm a bit? You are making his name more prominent than everything else.'

I did get niggled once when they asked me, purely out of courtesy, if I would mind them using a clip of me from *All Creatures*. I said it was fine by me, recorded the voice-over and left. When it went out on the television I realized they had synchronized the voice-over to the film clip making it look as though the character of James Herriot was talking about the girls on page three! A bit near the knuckle I felt.

A couple of days after the momentous news, as I pottered about the garden in the warm summer sun, vaguely trying to organize the youthful tangle of limbs around the swimming pool, the telephone rang. All fear of whatever news it might bring me temporarily alleviated, I belted inside.

'Yes?' I said breathlessly down the receiver.

'Is that Christopher Timothy?' asked a heavy guttural voice.

'Yes, speaking,' I said.

'It's the *Daily Mail* here,' the voice went on.

'Oh yes?' But I thought I wasn't to speak to the papers yet. 'Yes. The *Daily Mail* is it?' I said carefully.

'This James Herriot lark. Got a bit of good news then, haven't you?' Perhaps it was something arranged by the BBC. I did wish they had told me first.

'If you mean *All Creatures Great and Small*,' I replied, caught on the hop, 'then yes.'

'Gonna be good in it, then?' What a question to ask!

'I hope so,' I replied frostily, by now a bit alienated.

'Christopher Timothy hopes he is going to be good as James Herriot,' the voice said as though the man behind it was writing it down. 'Not a very riveting headline that, is it mate?' he queried.

'Well, what do you expect me to say?' I replied irritably.

'This here Herriot thing,' he went on, 'gonna make you a star?'

30

Was I always going to be asked questions like this?

'How should I know,' I said, by this time very irritated.

'Well, it bloody well ought to, mate!' Suddenly the guttural tones were dropped and I recognized the voice of my colleague from *Murder Most English*, Anton Rodgers.

chapter three

In further conversations with Bill Sellars we decided it would be a good idea if I were to meet the rest of the regular cast for *All Creatures Great and Small*. If we could briefly get to know one another before we started work then it might lessen the nervousness of the first few days' filming.

I also learnt that I need not have had the tortuous ten-day wait before hearing I had got the job. Several days before I was so thoughtfully informed by Simon, a number of people at the BBC had known. 'Have you phoned Chris Timothy?' they had asked whenever they bumped into Bill Sellars. 'Oh yes. I must do that,' a distracted Bill had always replied, and would then forget. The casting having been settled, with all the rigmarole of organization going on, it was a minor point that was overlooked.

One of the most satisfying moments of getting any job is the thud of the script falling through the letterbox. With feverish hands you tear open the heavy manilla package, whilst saying coolly, should anyone chance to be near, 'Ah . . . the script.' How gratifying it is to see your name printed opposite the character you've been asked to play. After all the commotion of getting the job it is the first time you see it in black and white. In this instance the postman had to abandon his bicycle and take to a van. After his several trips up and down the garden path, the hall table bulged with the strain of the stack of manilla packages upon it. This time too I received loads of congratulation cards from people from whom, in some cases, I had not heard in years.

A big bonus came a few days later when my agents called to say that the BBC wanted me to play one of the leads in a Play of the Month production of Arnold Wesker's *The Kitchen*. With three weeks to rehearse and record, it would fit in neatly before I went off to Yorkshire. In *The Kitchen* I was to play the character of Billy. The Irish accent I was to use would provide good practice at working with dialect in preparation for the Scottish accent I was to have for James Herriot.

In the event, of course, I did not use a Scottish accent. It was decided that the part was more accessible to everyone without. Perhaps it would have been too reminiscent of that long-running favourite *Dr Finlay's Casebook*. The Scots are at it again, people would think.

My vision of meeting the rest of the cast for *All Creatures* had been situated in some quiet room somewhere. We would all sit around drinking coffee, get to know each other, and perhaps relax. In the event, for some reason or other I was late. I belted into the room to find them all standing in line waiting for me. It must have been a joke on someone's part, for I was expected to parade up and down in front of them rather in the manner of the Queen inspecting the Guards.

First in line was Peter Davison, who would play Tristan. Peter is tall, blond and handsome in the way I wish I was. Both of us being exceedingly nervous, as a joke I said, 'No. Recast,' and passed on to the next person. Not until several days into the filming did he tell me that he had thought I really meant it. As soon as he could get away he had rushed to the telephone and called up his agent almost in tears. 'Christopher Timothy doesn't like me and wants me recast.' Being fairly new in the business it had never occurred to him that I might be feeling equally apprehensive, and was certainly not in a position to alter the casting.

Carol Drinkwater, who would be playing Helen Alderson, later James Herriot's wife, did a sort of mock curtsey and reminded me that when several years before I had been at the National Theatre she had supplemented her drama school grant by being a dresser there in the evenings. I'm afraid I only had a vague memory of it, but she had undoubtedly looked as beautiful then as she did now.

Then there was Mary Hignett, who would play Mrs Hall. An excellent choice; loving the period, she was always helpful with the etiquette of the 'thirties.

Of course there was Robert Hardy as Siegfried. We shook hands and said polite things. I was delighted to see him and greatly reassured to know that in a major undertaking we had such an old hand in the company.

All the productions for the BBC are rehearsed in a purpose-built block known in the trade as the Acton Hilton. There are several floors of large rehearsal rooms, three to each floor, with production offices attached. On top of it all is a large canteen and a terrace with a delightful view of railway sidings. Any actor or director who has ever worked for the BBC in the nine years since the block was built has passed through it. The canteen at lunchtime buzzes with actors greeting one another. The place is a paradise to the inveterate table-hopper and aids the speedy passage of gossip. Looking about, it occurred to me that the place must have taken over from Crewe Railway Station: in the old pre-television days when Britain was alive with theatres, hundreds of touring companies and variety acts would close on a Saturday night and spend Sunday travelling to the next venue; invariably it meant catching a connecting train at Crewe. On the platform, players who had not seen one another for years (or perhaps not since the week before) would meet up and exchange gossip and theatre news. 'You'll never guess who I saw at . . .' Crewe or Acton, the two are interchangeable, '. . . and I thought they'd died years ago!'

Several weeks prior to our cast meeting I had been at the Acton Hilton rehearsing *Murder Most English*. It was my first taste of being a regular in a series; it ran for seven episodes and I was greatly enjoying it. Whilst in the gents one day I stood next to Robert Hardy who at that time I didn't know. *Edward VII* was then being repeated. My family were glued to it, and as Prince Albert we all thought Robert Hardy smashing; so I told him. He was obviously pleased and politely said thank-you.

However many times you have been congratulated on a piece of work, it is still gratifying even years later when someone says how much they've enjoyed it. I think of our milkman who volunteered one morning after I had appeared in *The Two Ronnies*:

'Saw you on telly last night. Do you mind a bit of constructive criticism?' 'No, not at all,' I replied, beginning to preen. 'I thought you were bloody awful!'

Several weeks later when I was mooted for the part of James Herriot, Robert Hardy, who would have already been asked to play Siegfried, remembering my earnest congratulations proffered in the gents said, 'Oh yes! He's splendid! He'll do very well.' Nice of him when he didn't know my work!

Robert Hardy was always enthusiastic and encouraging right from the start. I learnt later that it was he who insisted I should have equal billing with him. 'After all,' he argued, 'whoever plays James Herriot, a "name" or not, must have star billing.'

The meeting was of course far too brief. I only managed to have a few minutes with him before being led away to discuss 'in depth' the relationship between Helen and James Herriot. A bit premature, I remember thinking. They barely meet in the first episode. It is not until several episodes later that they get married.

I ought perhaps to clarify a point about Robert Hardy's name It seems a bit formal to constantly refer to him using both the the christian and the surname. Yet Robert is not his real name. Known to everyone as Tim, Robert is only a 'professional' name. His family, friends and work-mates still call him Tim, whilst on the credits 'Robert' rolls by.

With my name being Christopher Timothy and the two of us working together, there could be confusion. Early on in the filming he was most insistent that the production team call him Robert to avoid this. Sometimes, in reply to the cameraman's 'I wonder if you could move over this way, Tim,' the sharp retort of 'Robert!' was a bit abrupt. In a few days, however, it certainly had its effect.

Timothy is of course a good Welsh surname, both my parents being from sound Welsh stock. My mother's background was the Empire Administrator type. Her parents, the Hailstones, lived in a house called 'Tan Rhiw' which, translated, means 'halfway up a steep hill'. It always struck me as being singularly appropriate for that is exactly where it is. Very good for tobagganing, I remember. My father came from nearby Corwyn where my mother, having studied briefly as a dancer, gave dancing lessons.

Because of the war and my parents' divorce my mother, brother and I lived mostly with her parents until I was thirteen, when we moved across the border to nearby Shrewsbury. My maternal grandparents also had a flat in London where for short periods we would live from time to time. My grandfather remained in London throughout the war as an ARP man, and it was in the flat that he died of cancer in 1950. A quiet, dignified man with short velvety hair that we kids loved to stroke, and round metal-framed glasses, he never interfered in our lives. But he was always supportive to my mother who faced the difficult task of bringing up two small boys alone; the more difficult for her being divorced at a time when divorce carried a stigma. Certainly it seems to me unfair that the strongest memory I have now of my grandfather should be one of childhood chastisement. 'Your grandfather died because you were rude,' someone once told me.

About the time when my grandfather was subsiding into his terminal illness, it was my birthday. Selfishly I insisted on having a party. This was arranged in a room at the Kensington Odeon. The noise of twenty or so loud, overexcited little boys disturbed the patrons of the cinema below, resulting in several complaints and the arrival of a reporter from the local paper, desperate then as now for a story I suppose. Perhaps it seemed a good idea at the time or perhaps I truly did believe it, although I think it may just have been the influence of the many films I had seen where the good guy with the pretty girl got the better of the nasty villain; for I said, when asked what I wanted to be when I grew up, 'I want to be an actor.'

Whatever the reason was, and wishful thinking as it sometimes seemed, I stuck to it. On reflection it seems to be the only direction I had, linking together and giving some sense of purpose to my distinctly raggle-taggle childhood.

'You'll never be an actor,' said the prep-school master to me when I was twelve. 'I will, I will!' I replied.

'Don't worry, Timothy. We'll get you on stage at the Old Vic if it kills us,' said an encouraging master at my grammar school.

Having finally become an actor, surviving the disbelief and downright lack of encouragement I met throughout my school-days, I was not going to fail at the last hurdle, the hurdle of success.

Sue has always been a great boost. Whenever a job has come up I would like to do but feel I should avoid because of the small salary, she has said without hesitation, 'If you want to do it, then you must. We'll manage somehow,' and somehow things usually have worked out.

I should add that although the staff at my various schools were dismissive of my wish to be an actor it was probably only a general reflection of their despair at my scholastic abilities. There were so many misconceptions then about life in the theatre that it was a very easy ambition for schoolmasters to take a swipe at. My mother's despair took another form: anything, she thought, so long as he is happy and doesn't come to the sticky end his school career threatens.

My father, a shadowy figure throughout my childhood, who occasionally materialized to take both my brother and myself out for the odd Sunday, after being a military chaplain had become a broadcaster. He became famous as the straight-man in *The Goon Show*, a fact of which I was inordinately proud. Needless to say my bragging of this to school-mates was met with total disbelief. Not much credence was given to anything I professed! They had never recovered from my declaration that I was a boxer. This avowal was based on a brief sparring match I had when I was seven; the other boy was distinctly weedy and had melted away from my first blow leaving me the ring. At prep school, after my unwise assertion that I could box, I was set against the champion. This was quite another matter. Although I could bounce around and stab the air in fair imitation of Sugar Ray Robinson and had the promise of doing well, faced with the reality I very quickly decided life and limb were worth far more than any fleeting victory and dubious popularity. To the jeers of my erstwhile supporters, with a record-breaking leap over the ropes, I abandoned the ring.

When I was eighteen my father invited me down to stay in London with him and his wife. For a couple of heady weeks he whisked me around in and out of Broadcasting House, where he worked, and introduced me to as many of his influential friends as he could. They must have thought I was pretty unpromising material, gawky and spotty as I was, for the constant advice was, 'Go to drama school.' This is a polite way of saying, 'There's not much I can do, but three years knocking you into shape might help.' At that time, unlike now, it was possible not to go to drama school but to join a company in the most menial position and work your way up, serving a kind of apprenticeship. If no one snapped me up, my visit at least made into a reality what had just been a fantasy. I returned to Shrewsbury more determined than ever.

How very different schools are now to the way they were even twenty years ago when I was a pupil. Now all the Arts are encouraged as an aid to the growth of expression and child development. It would have been unthinkable for me to return home from school proudly clutching a picture I had spent all day painting as my son Simon does. One of Simon's pictures was of William the Conqueror waving his sword, covered in blood and with arrows everywhere; this gory portrait was entitled 'William the Conqueror at the Battle of Hastings after he had fallen in a rose bush'. With this kind of logic everything is possible!

One of the great things about being an actor and therefore frequently before the public is that when as a child you mutter, 'I'll show you!' chances are you really can. It is unfair that you can become the world's most eminent neuro surgeon and no one you fell foul of at school might ever know. Since doing *All Creatures Great and Small* many people I lost contact with years ago have been in touch. One of the most gratifying of these was the maths master at Shrewsbury Grammar.

Known as Batty Bland, wearing a hearing aid and waving a stick, he was a natural target for schoolboy japes. The type of eccentric who could only be found in English academic circles, he would pronounce to his dissolute class:

If you don't understand
put up your hand
and ask Batty Bland.

If the ill-disciplined ragging reached too intolerable a pitch he would simply turn off his hearing aid.

The letter I received from him a short while ago I found deeply moving. In it he wrote that I had been 'a victim of an outdated educational system'. All those years spent being a victim! But it is an encouragement in the education of my own children.

Always agitating for work when I was unemployed, I would write ceaseless letters. Two schools of thought exist over this. There are those actors who hold that directors and producers must get so many it is useless to add to them and better to leave it to your agent; others, probably the majority, think it worthwhile writing regardless. I take the second view and must carry it to an extreme. When *All Creatures Great and Small* is over I shall most likely pick up where I left off, maybe a bit more selectively this time. I don't believe in leaving anything to chance.

In the past the act of writing has certainly helped alleviate the tension of hanging around waiting for the next job. Initially I would go through a copy of the *Radio Times* and write to everybody. Frequently the letters would be ignored or sometimes the reply would come back, 'This man is a stunt-man. He is of absolutely no use to you.' When I was broke I would write on anything that came to hand. The backs of old envelopes, flyleaves torn from books, the backs of which would have that curious marbled effect in either brown or purple. On reflection it seems like sacrilege, but the letters certainly looked different! It was always dispiriting when they produced no reply, or when the standard roneod acknowledgement came back, but I soon became used to that. For every other batch of letters I wrote I always ended up with at least one job.

One time, when lack of work was driving me crazy, I made up letters that looked like the traditional anonymous poison-pen letter. Carefully I would construct messages from words cut from newspapers and glue them to the page. It used to take me for ever but the result looked fairly startling. 'Christopher Timothy' I would cut from an old *TV Times*. 'Have you seen Christopher Timothy in . . .' or 'What about Christopher Timothy for . . .' the higgledy-piggledy letters ran.

Quietly going about my all-engrossing task one afternoon and doing a spot of babysitting at the same time, the phone rang. Simon, then aged three, picked up the receiver. 'Hello,' he said, 'oh yes . . . Dick Lester,' I heard him say. I flew across the room almost horizontal to the floor. I caught the phone just as Simon was letting the receiver fall back on to the hook.

Dick Lester is a big film director. He had made the Beatles' films, and amongst the many he went on to do were the recent remakes of *The Three Musketeers*. At that time he was setting up a film of one of the highly successful *Flashman* novels. He had naturally been a recipient of one of my many patchwork letters.

'Christopher Timothy here,' I gasped down the phone.

'I have Dick Lester for you,' said an efficient-sounding secretarial voice, followed by the click of the switchboard.

'OK Timothy. Drop the scissors,' came Dick Lester's voice. Sure enough, dangling from my inert hand was a pair of scissors. 'Saw you on television last night,' the voice went on without giving me a moment to recover from my surprise. '*Three Sisters*. Liked it. Know your work. But even shot through gauze you're too *old*.'

With my letters I had hoped to take them by surprise, but the result had been unexpected. I don't think I composed another one that day. Dazed, I remembered too that I was only twenty-seven.

But now, at last, the moment for departure had arrived. I was to stay with a vet in Yorkshire and watch hard as he went about his business.

chapter four

Leaving Heathrow we were to fly north and fetch up in the village of Leyburn, a greyish but typical market town in the heart of Herriot country. With me was the first of our directors, Terry Dudley, and the production assistant Janet Radenkovic. They would deposit me at the vet with whom I was to stay and then go off for a final reconnoitre of the locations where, a week later, we would begin filming.

As always I was dressed practically. I looked just the part for a 'television star' setting out with the film unit to do some realistic down-to-earth shots. Faded denims, white moccasin shoes and the obligatory dark glasses. Goodness knows why: I had never worn them in my life and hated doing so now. I can only offer in defence the fact that it was a warm summer's day.

Speedily we arrived at the vet's and were greeted by one of his two sons. A very affable bloke of fifteen to sixteen, he apologized for his father being out on a call and told us that his mother, not expecting us so soon, was still at a committee meeting. Gracefully he entertained us and wheeled in a tea-trolley whose shelves literally overflowed with goodies. Being used to a cup of tea and a rather sorry looking biscuit, I was ill-prepared for the abundance of sandwiches and cakes that would have better fed twenty than three. It was my first taste of the generous hospitality I was to receive.

Halfway through my second chocolate cake, into the room strode the vet himself, Jack Watkinson. In his wellington boots, tweed jacket and habitual bowtie he appeared to be everybody's image of the country vet. To meet him was deeply reassuring. From the start we got on well and I was delighted he was to be one of the two consultant vets on the series. I don't think he was equally reassured. My Londoner's idea of what to wear in the country must have looked ridiculous to his practical eye. As soon

43

as tea was over and Terry and Janet had left, he brusquely said if I was ready perhaps I would go and change as it was time to be off about the practice. Pushing the dark glasses to the bottom of my suitcase for ever and hastily pulling on the sparkling pair of wellingtons so recently purchased at enormous cost in London, I belted downstairs and joined him in the hall.

I must say now I don't think I could have had a better coach. Always compassionate and endlessly patient, within a very short time he eased me into the realities of a country practice. As willing and (more or less!) capable as I turned out to be as a student, I don't think he was ever quite able to forget I was an actor.

However much you immerse yourself in another's work, however much you forget yourself, at the end of the day you are only an actor. In that is your strength. But there are times when, forgetting, you are brought up short. Some years earlier I was in Singapore to film *The Virgin Soldiers*, based on Leslie Thomas' book. Set in the 1950s it was about the experiences of a group of young men who whilst doing their National Service get caught up in the atrocities of the Malayan war. Larking about in a shop with some other young actors at the end of the day's shoot, and forgetting we were still in our costumes of army uniform, a voice suddenly said, 'You sure are lucky just playing at being soldiers.' We turned to see the speaker was a man considerably younger than us, wearing a GI uniform; he was on leave from Vietnam. His eyes were middle-aged.

The first call with Jack was to a woman whose cat had bad breath. This was something that only happened in cartoons, I thought. Jack was able to resolve this with a quick tooth extraction and a word to the owner about the cat's diet. Afterwards he told me that over and over again he had to deal with the psychology of the owner whose loving but misguided care had resulted in their pet's misfortune. Fifty per cent of his veterinary skill was expended in treating the owner rather than the animal – a good lesson for understanding James Herriot's treatment of Mrs Pumphrey and the infamous Tricki Woo.

The next stop was to geld a racehorse at the stables. A massive creature with what I felt to be the power of twenty of us, he stood nervously pawing the ground and snorting. Goodness, I thought, rather Jack than me. With the nifty application of a local anaesthetic and a sort of vice with teeth that seared shut the flesh as it cut, within seconds the would-be stallion was no more. He looked as surprised as I did.

'You can take 'em home and eat 'em. They be grand to eat,' said the groom, giving a prod with his foot to the part of the horse that now lay neatly on the ground before us.

'Oh yes.' I gave a sort of half laugh that committed me neither way.

'Go on. They're delicious. The wife'll have 'em if you don't want 'em.'

Dubiously glancing down I surveyed the proffered mass that glistened in the afternoon sun. Given a nudge by Jack I realized that my all too apparent naivety was not being sent up as I'd suspected. Far from it – I was being offered a compliment.

'That's very kind of you,' I hastily replied, sounding as though I had a plum in my mouth. 'No! No! I couldn't possibly. You have them.' And I meant it.

My previous encounters with horses had been none too auspicious. Like most actors at interviews I was only too ready to answer in the affirmative when asked if there was a particular skill I could perform. 'What? Walk a tight-rope over the Niagara Falls?' I would say settling back in my chair with a dismissive laugh. 'Why! I do it every day before breakfast.'

'Speak fluent Hungarian? No problem! My grandmother was Hungarian.'

When the stakes are high, suddenly there is nothing you cannot do.

Riding is one of the most common skills required of an actor. Although I had never had to interview for an epic film I went to do in Ireland (which shall remain nameless), it had been assumed I could ride. A slight misunderstanding, for a quick read of contemporary history of a thousand years ago had told me that very few of the men of the period actually rode. If they did it was only on ponies, the vast majority going on foot. Since no one had said anything I had assumed my character was to be one of those, and in the interim never bothered to learn.

The trip to Ireland should have prepared me for the realities of an epic film that goes wrong. A 'bomber' at the box-office, the film rapidly disappeared with only intermittent late-night television screenings to remind one of the full horrors of it all. I have every admiration for the film's director, with whom I had worked before. Even with his considerable skill, through circumstances way beyond his control, the whole enterprise was doomed from the start.

Vivien Merchant, the film's leading lady, mutely showed me her script when I asked her what she thought of it. She had run through every page of her heavy dialogue with a red pencil, neatly crossing it all out: an explicit gesture. And mute she remained. When the film came out, other than smiling, nodding or looking cross, I don't think she said a word.

Landing at Dublin airport, waving goodbye to the other actors on the flight who were all over to film *Where's Jack*, the picture with Tommy Steele, I looked for the car I had been told would meet me and whizz me off to the location. Nothing. I settled down to wait. Hour after hour ticked by with still no sign of a car as, one after another, the airport lights switched off. The silence was only broken by the rhythmical swishing of the cleaner's broom. 'You still here?' she said, looking up as her broom hit an unexpected obstacle that was me.

'Yes,' I snapped somewhat peevishly. No one had told me the whereabouts of the film unit. The most terrible thing of all was that I could not for the life of me remember what the film was called. Because it was late in the evening I could not call up the London offices to find out such details. Besides, smartly dressed as I was, I had but 7/6d in my pocket.

'Oh well . . . never you mind, dearie.' And she waddled off trailing her broom, making patterns in the dust as she went.

'That's a great comfort,' I muttered angrily to her retreating back, pulling my lightweight summer casuals about me to ward off the chill of the night. I did mind awfully. What the devil was I to do? A night spent in lonely vigilance outside a closed airport didn't seem a pleasant prospect. But there was nothing for it.

Just as I was settling down for an uncomfortable night on my suitcases and putting on a sweater I had found in one of them, she came flip-flopping back.

'I've found a taxi that will take you into Dublin and the driver says he knows a nice hotel where you can stay,' she announced.

'But I haven't got a bean,' I told her.

'Don't you go worrying your head about things like that now, Just you explain and they'll sort something out, a nice young lad like you.' I rose to my feet in gratitude. 'Anyway, the driver's a brother of mine,' she added as an afterthought.

The taxi-driver and the people at the hotel could not have been kinder. Deeply tired as I was by that time, after a good meal, they insisted I go to bed and sleep, not give it another thought. The driver must have worked throughout what was left of the night. The next morning I was informed that he had discovered not only what the film was called, but also where it was filming. An official car was waiting to take me the two-hour drive out to the location. Not a penny would any of them take in remuneration. It was their pleasure, they insisted. As soon as I got my expenses I sent them a cheque.

Still riddled with fatigue I staggered from the car. I was in a field situated in the middle of nowhere which the driver assured me was the location.

This can't be the right place, I thought as I surveyed the vast green and undulating expanse that seemed to have been empty from the beginning of time. With a cheery honk of the hooter, the car disappeared over a hillock – leaving me, suitcases piled at my feet, engulfed in the eerie country silence which was broken only by the occasional birdsong, a solitary butterfly for company.

'I've done it again!' I groaned out loud to the fronds of grass that remained unstirred, not even a gentle breeze to set them rippling in response.

'People of Ireland, where are you?' I shouted into the emptiness.

'Over 'ere, mate,' said a disembodied voice that froze me in my tracks.

'Where?' I said weakly, unable to discern from which direction the voice had come. Tales of leprechauns sprang to mind. But surely not with a cockney accent!

'Let me give you a hand with those bags.' The stocky bejeaned figure of a film technician rounded a small incline.

'By God, am I glad to see you!' I said, relieved in the way Stanley must have been to meet Livingstone.

'Is this the location?' I asked feeling rather foolish at my question.

'You can say that again! You Christopher Timothy?' To my nod he continued. 'We've been expecting you.'

I wasn't even sarcastic as, suitcases in hand, he led me round the incline from behind which he had just come. There, laid out in a bowl before me, were a couple of hundred people. The caravans, arc lamps and champing horses made it look like a fairground.

'Nice to see you,' said the director, striding over to where I stood, my suitcases once again littering the ground around me.

'We're in a bit of a rush, so as soon as you're costumed perhaps we can go straight into the first shot. It'll be you, David Hemmings, and half a dozen others riding down this slope here, over the brook and up the hill on the other side.'

'But . . . but . . .' I stammered. 'I can't ride. No one told me I would have to ride.'

'Can't you?'

'And I'm so tired I don't think I could even sit on a chair,' I added.

'Tell you what we'll do. Go and grab some lunch and then we will send you out with one of the stuntmen. By the end of the day you'll be riding! We'll do the shot first thing tomorrow.'

Sure enough, the stuntman set me on a pony, which was reassuring, but far from being the crash course in horsemanship

I had anticipated. For two hours he merely led me on a long rein round and round in a circle, never letting me go faster than walking pace.

Well, it won't be too demanding then, I thought, as finally I curled my aching limbs up under the blanket, snuggling down at last to blissful sleep. Even *I* can ride like that . . .

At dawn the next day I was in the make-up caravan.

'Oh dear, this wig's a bit tight,' said the make-up girl, jamming some more pins into the shaggy blonde thing that perched on top of my head. 'It's only because it's new,' she went on, a strained expression on her face as she attempted to yank the thing back down to my ears. 'It'll soon relax.'

'It's only because it's new. It'll soon relax,' said the wardrobe girl as she watched me struggle into the iron clamps that were my rust-coloured suede trousers and jerkin, and called for an assistant to help transport me into the field outside.

'Ah, good morning Chris, feeling better?' the director cheerily asked. 'That's your horse over there,' and he pointed at what seemed to my startled eye more like the mountains of Donegal than a horse.

With the aid of half a dozen prop-men I was soon precariously ensconced on the summit, the reins gripped for dear life by my cast-iron gauntlets.

'When in doubt, hang on to the pommel,' the stuntman had told me.

'This is your spear,' said a prop-man, handing up a metal and wooden thing the size of a rugger-post, the weight of it nearly unseating me.

'And this is your shield.' I stared with horror at a wooden disc the size of a circus ring.

'No. Please!' I begged. 'I've only got two hands.'

The designer was called over for a quick consultation.

'But if I've got a sword in one hand and a shield in the other how do I steer the horse?' I urged.

'Everyone else manages quite well,' he replied tartly. 'The Irish have been doing it for thousands of years.'

49

'I can't even move in this costume.'

'Well, it was made to the measurements you gave us, so I can't help that.'

'I know. Just give me a couple of days and I promise I'll carry the shield then.' I nearly wept.

'Oh, all right then,' he relented. 'But just for today, mind.'

The finished film distinctly shows but one horseman not carrying a shield, a sort of wobbly red blob meandering its way at some distance from the tightly packed little band of riders, carefully picking its way over the brook it potters along where the others canter. A leap nearly unseating it, it finishes up some several yards from where the group have come to rest some minutes before.

Later on during the three months I was filming, my costume having expanded in all the right places, and having pal'd up a bit with my gargantuan horse, growing cocky I asked the director if for a certain shot I couldn't dismount the way I had seen in all those cowboy movies. Like Steve McQueen would, I wanted to get off the horse by throwing my leg over the front and sliding down, as opposed to what I felt to be the more riding-school method of a leg thrown over the back and the careful removal of the other foot from the stirrup.

The sequence was of the leader of the heroic army delivering to us a good blood-stirring speech that having pepped us up would stimulate us into galloping across the field below at full tilt.

The field had previously been a lake surrounded by acres of bog. In the way that film companies do, at spectacular expense, the bog had been covered over with fibre-glass and surmounted with turf; so the seemingly solid ground extended down to the water. However, the artificial land thus created was not as solid as it appeared to the camera; still treacherous and water-logged. The horses were very wary of it. Having cajoled my reluctant mount at speed to the water's edge, with spirit I threw my leg over the front of the horse to hurl myself to the ground. Unfortunately I forgot to remove my other foot from the stirrup. My legs entangled, I plummeted perpendicularly into the squelchy

50

mire, my head buried up to the neck. Only the quick-wittedness of a fellow actor who, realizing I was unable to move, dragged me clear, saved me from death by drowning.

The camera is very good at making things look what they are not. For the cricket match sequence in *All Creatures* we used a field so bumpy that even a hundred steamrollers would have had no effect. The story required the pitch to be by no means perfect, but this was ridiculous. 'But we can't play on that!' I protested. But we did. Well used to the world of make-believe created by the camera and the judicious snip of the editor's scissors, this seemed to me just to be making life unnecessarily hard. I was brought up to think Yorkshire and cricket synonymous. There must be a suitable field somewhere in Yorkshire for us to use, I thought. But other factors stepped in. Time and convenience cost money. It is sometimes cheaper to stay put, to be able to go on to the next set-up faster, to get more into the day. In the sequence that ran on television no one would have suspected for a minute that the field was other than mildly pitted. I might have drowned in what looked like solid ground to the few cinema-goers who saw the film done in Ireland, but with a nifty snip from the editor, only those of us who were on location knew that.

Maybe it was all in preparation for the extraordinary directorial wizardry that was needed from halfway through the first series of *All Creatures*. But more of that to follow!

Our consultant vet, Jack Watkinson, found the apparently inexplicable antics of the film crew unfathomable for the first few weeks.

A stickler as we all were for absolute authenticity, he hovered watchfully behind the camera, checking that in every detail our handling of the animals was correct. As we came to appreciate the methods in his handling of livestock that sometimes seemed at variance with our own citified views, so he learnt the technicalities of working with the camera. Soon he was able to ask of the director if something was 'in shot' or not with all the casualness of years of experience. We in our turn learnt not to mutter

51

dark things about the RSPCA as Jack quietly and compassionately went about his business.

It was not very compassionate when, fresh from London and only two hours into my new life as a vet, Jack and I went on to meet my first cow 'in depth', as you might say. For Jack it was very routine job. The cow had to be cleansed of afterbirth. Without much ado, he rolled up his sleeves and plunged deep into the rear of it. Watching him from the side of my eyes, my head averted, I reminded myself that the scripts for the series called repeatedly for Herriot to do exactly the same. This undoubtedly would be faked, the camera cutting from a shot of my face to Jack's arms actually doing it. No room for squeamishness: if I was to see Jack frequently doing this on the set then I had better get used to watching him now. The afterbirth – which I am certain I have no need to describe, sufficient to say words like 'unpleasant' suddenly lose all meaning – lay on the floor. The two farm hands stood about enjoying my discomfiture, as I forced my head back to watch what Jack was doing.

'You want to take that home with you. Makes a lovely pie,' one said whilst nudging the other.

Goodness! do they eat everything in the country? I thought, desperately trying to make myself look at the awful afterbirth as though I had seen it a dozen times before. After the episode with the horse-gelding I was none too certain. Again, in response, I settled for a sort of uneasy half-laugh that would not commit me either way. Anxiously I looked to Jack for support but, busy as he was with the cow, he remained oblivious. I looked at the farm hands again, hoping to find an indication of their sincerity or otherwise. They remained pokerfaced and, although I was positive I had seen them nudge each other, my mind flew to the strange foods I had heard of. I knew of haggis, and I had often seen brains listed on restaurant menus. I knew now of the truth about the innocuous-sounding 'sweet-breads'. But cows' afterbirth? They couldn't really mean it. Luckily, the farm hands, unable to suppress their merriment at my evident consternation, broke into laughter. I was just joining in when Jack turned to me and said, 'Right. Up you go.'

'Sorry?' I said, wondering if I had heard correctly, the laughter dying on my lips.

'Might as well break the ice, so to speak. Up you go,' and he nodded in the direction of the cow, leaving me in no doubt as to what he meant.

In answer to those letters in the *Radio Times* that ask 'Don't vets do anything else?' the answer is that vets do, but a lot of time is spent in exactly this way. Cows constantly need cleansing of the afterbirth or help with some minor readjustment to the works. For the country vet it is common enough to do half a dozen a day. The vet doesn't give it a thought and neither does the cow.

To the other type of letter saying, 'It's a real vet whose arms we see,' I can only reply that that's how I thought it would be, but I'm afraid not! It doesn't require much concentration to tell that in this particular instance the camera does not lie.

I may be a bit blasé now, a few hundred cows later, but when Jack first ordered me up, I was terrified. The farm hands, hardly able to contain themselves with delight at the shades of green my face must have gone, stood back crossing their arms with an unspoken 'OK, let's see what you can do,' in the way they did to the young James Herriot forty years before.

Breathing heavily, I removed my shirt. Oh no! Horrors! I had underneath a tee shirt proudly emblazoned with the words 'Daily Mirror'. My humiliation was complete.

Bravely pushing aside the doubt he must have had, Jack said, 'OK. Now I've put two suppositories quite deep inside and I want you to fetch one of them out.' Gritting my teeth, I plunged.

I have been subsequently told of the horrendous things that can happen to your arm whilst it is so deployed; of the muscles that suddenly clamp shut holding your arm for ever and painfully locked in position; of the all too easy turn up the wrong passage. Thankfully, on my first trip, none of these things occurred. After what was by the clock only a momentary panic and what to me seemed endless searching my hand found the suppository. Firmly taking hold of it, my ordeal over, I drew out my arm in triumph and presented it to Jack.

'Good. Now put it back again.' He would give no mercy. The cow remained unmoved, chewing dreamily on her cud.

'Nothing quite like it!' I joked through clenched teeth, as I thrust back in.

'Now you can give yourself a good scrubbing under that tap over there,' said Jack, smiling for the first time. 'I think we'll make a vet of you yet.'

That day he made me go up another four cows. 'There's not much to be worried about when you've done that,' he told me. Giving myself a final scrub down I reflected I had well and truly 'broken the ice'.

Barring accidents and the odd excursion up the wrong passage that leaves you covered from head to foot in what rose-growers go wild about, it is an extraordinary sensation, not at all unpleasant, and surprisingly clean.

As a kid it had always seemed tiresome to have to trail through ditches of disinfectant that appeared to be placed round every bend in the road in the countryside. Vaguely hearing reports of foot-and-mouth disease on the radio, I was inattentive. Even as an adult, although I always followed the country code as advertised on television, the realities of farming and animal care were a long way removed. By the time we were all only a few days into the series we had become acutely conscious of the need for it.

When we returned home that first evening we were filthy. Jack had a broom in his yard with which, under a flowing tap and with the aid of a tray of disinfectant, he would scrub his boots until they sparkled. The mounds of dirty laundry that heaped up at the end of every day were whisked away by his wife Jess.

In the series we seemed to be forever washing ourselves. Because it was not always practical to have running water and a sink in the studio, we would sometimes have to mime the action whilst the camera shot only our top half. On occasions the floor assistant would kneel under the camera holding up to us a bucket in which we could splash around and make the appropriate sounds.

Recently on a radio comedy show I heard a very funny sketch,

The residents of Skeldale, the fictitious name of the house in which the Farnon–Herriot practice is based, were returning home after a long day working about the place. Automatically, one after another, they went to the sink, and the greetings of 'Hello James,' 'Ah, good evening Siegfried,' 'Good evening Tristan,' 'Hello James. Hello Siegfried,' 'Good evening dogs,' 'Hello Mrs Hall,' 'Good evening Siegfried, James, Tristan,' and so on were drowned out by the sound of sloshing water and the scrubbing brush. It hit the nail right on the head. A bottle of hand cream for every episode!

A far cry from when as a young actor at the National Theatre I actually played a fountain, and not nearly as painful either. For twenty-five minutes night after night I knelt motionless. Along with a number of equally ambitious young actors, known as the Inanimates, we posed as statuary throughout Franco Zeffirelli's controversial production of Shakespeare's *Much Ado About Nothing*. The theatrical effect was achieved by a figure that seemed to be part of the scenery suddenly moving, thereby commenting on the action of the play. The fountain that had been standing there, looking for all the world like a real stone fountain would, all of a sudden, put up an umbrella. It was agony! Our padded stone-coloured costumes would be dripping with sweat when we left the stage. On rehearsal days I would drag myself from my bed thinking, Oh no! I can't face it, and long for it to be all over. However, for every Inanimate you played you got paid another pound a performance. I wanted that money!

I don't think Zeffirelli ever even noticed that we were made of flesh and blood and not mechanical, so intent was he on achieving the effect.

Some time later after I had done the film *The Mulberry Bush*, which had set some young actors, myself included, on the road to becoming established, I went to do some dubbing for Zeffirelli's famous film *Romeo and Juliet*, which was then nearing completion. I was to provide some of the 'oohs' and 'aahs', and the one-line exclamations of the small parts.

As I walked into the studio Zeffirelli said to me in front of the

55

small gathering of some really distinguished actors, 'Hello Chris, I understand you're one of England's most exciting young actors at the moment.' Embarrassed by what I felt to be a gibe, I played along.

'That's right, Franco,' I said airily.

'Now I want you to scream for me,' he continued.

Whilst he recorded I screamed.

'No, no,' he said. 'Not in that actor's way. I want a real blood-curdling scream.'

So I screamed again.

'That's better,' he said, 'but give me more.'

I screamed again. Again and again he made me scream. Unprotected by the actor's technique that allows you to scream and yell without danger to your voice, within minutes it had gone husky. Minutes later it had disappeared altogether.

'Well, I think I have a scream that maybe I can use,' said Zeffirelli. 'Thank you Chris.'

With my voice in tatters I was unable to do the next three days' work for which I had been booked.

Zeffirelli is one of the greatest directors, giving to the world wonderful, stylish and individualistic productions on film and for the stage. Maybe it was just my fancy, but somewhere I must have fallen foul of him, hitting the ruthless streak which makes him the creative force he is. With the tendency I have for hurling myself into whatever is going on, it made me acutely conscious of where to draw the line, and of the need to exercise a little self-protection. Meanwhile, what was a cow or two?

Next day, one of the many calls we made was to a cow that had bloat. I learnt cows don't eat the grass all in one go, seeing, chewing, swallowing and dispatching as you might expect. Swallowing the grass, it goes into a sort of subsidiary stomach from which the cow can then regurgitate it and give it a final chew at leisure before dispatching it down the usual channels for ever. On occasion the regurgitating mechanism gets blocked up, resulting in the cow becoming bloated with wind. This cow had blown up to twice its normal size and died. Jack made me tap it. The cow's hide felt as taut as a drum skin. In such instances the only thing for it is to make a puncture, deflating it like a balloon. This we did. The gas that rushes out is inflammable. I read in the newspapers recently of a farmer in Germany who was suing for the replacement of the whole of his farm. A cow had gone off with a bang, and the whole animal had ignited, burning down the buildings. This fact gave perspective to the sequence in *All Creatures Great and Small* when a farmer casually lights a match as Tristan is puncturing a cow.

I had been led to believe that farmers were not emotionally involved with their animals. I don't know where I got that from. I suppose I thought familiarity bred a kind of casualness – something I obviously hadn't thought out.

The farmers, bachelor brothers, who owned this particular bloated cow, were obviously deeply upset. Shy and retiring, their world was centred around the farm, the gates of which they only left when they had to. Sometimes we did meet up with an uncaring farmer, someone who had gone into farming because it seemed the only thing to do. After treating their animals Jack would mutter furiously about callousness.

As we went about the practice Jack would, if he felt it of interest to the various animal-owners, explain who I was. Often the people we visited had known the real James Herriot and they would stand back nodding appreciation. At other times he would just let them assume what they wanted. Maybe my ineptness would not be so apparent and my presence was not in need of justification.

Trundling along the road one morning we were hailed by a farmer. Leaving the car and following him across a field, we came upon a cow standing up to its neck in a sort of quagmire, the remains of a dried-up water pool. The farmer informed us that the cow had been there for twenty-four hours. Unable to extract itself, its struggling had only succeeded in further wedging it in. Throwing boards across the mud in the time-honoured way, although enabling us to move across, otherwise proved ineffectual. At a loss as to what next to do and looking about us, Jack suddenly saw a building site some several fields away. Rushing over to it, he pursuaded the men to bring over a tractor-like crane they were using. Slipping and sliding on banks of mud it seemed only minutes until, with a gurgling sound, the crane would disappear too. A machine that vast we would never be able to extricate. Perched on the pincer-like crane, Jack was flown aloft until he dangled just above the cow. Guided by the man at the controls, carefully the pincers dug in the mud. Finding where they hoped the cow's bony haunches might be, they gently clamped shut. With a squelching sound the mud reluctantly yielded the cow, which was by this time in a state of deep shock, and the tractor dragged it to safety.

As Jack brushed the mud from himself, his only comment to the farmer who had stood by hands in pockets was, 'For goodness sake get some fencing put round.' He strode away back to his car.

During the week I stayed at the Watkinsons', there was not a call to which Jack went without taking me. Although very tentative about waking me, with a gentle tap on the door at five o' clock one morning, he whispered that there was a calving he had to attend. Within minutes we were driving through the stunning dawn light.

The calving was going to be difficult. Reaching into the womb, Jack tied a rope around the feet of the unborn calf. It took all of his considerable strength to pull it out. With a great thud the calf hit the decks. A split-second later he had thrown himself on to it, scraping away the mucus that covered it, pounding its chest to make the lungs go and, when that didn't work, giving the calf mouth-to-mouth recuscitation. It did the trick; minutes later the calf rather wonkily sat up. There in the dawn light at the beginning of what promised to be a beautiful day it was a very moving scene, one in which we all shared. For some moments we stood still just gazing at the new-born calf.

Breaking the spell, Jack matter-of-factly began to clear up. Joining him, I said, 'Don't ever tell me that vets don't get emotionally involved.' From his face, and the farmer's too, you could see that even after the many such births they had attended they had never lost the wonder of it.

Looking about Jack's smartly equipped surgery and thinking of his fast Jaguar parked outside, I reflected that the developments in medicine since the time in which the Herriot books are set must have greatly eased the burden. 'Not a bit of it,' I was told. 'All these advances mean is that the vet can move faster. As a result he has to pack into his working day more than he would have in the past.'

Nor had anything replaced the brute strength required. Both Jack and his wife, who would often assist him in the surgery, forever seemed to be humping about the inert bodies of quite large animals. Of the strength needed by Jack there was no doubt. Many was the time I saw him lift prostrate cattle to their feet or hold a horse firmly, the better to examine it. All helped by the enormous intake of food: nipping back home for a snack lunch was not a snack in any sense of the word I had known. The kitchen table would be overflowing with pies and cold-cuts from a dozen different joints of meat. Standing by and watching as Jack worked, for the first time in my life I put on weight, but it was weight I would need if I was to play a vet.

Jack's skill and strength combined to make me sometimes feel like a rather puny weed trailing along behind him. And my ego was not exactly boosted when we called in to see a bull that in a few days we would be using for filming.

The farmer who greeted us was a vast, jovial man the size of a house. Even he was no preparation for his bull; a solid wall of muscle, it towered above us. Firmly placed behind the sort of bars which might contain a herd of rhino, it very definitely gave me second thoughts about wanting to be an actor. Within a few minutes, though, the farmer having insisted despite all impressions to the contrary the bull was soft and gentle, I was inside the cage scratching its ears as it rubbed its head up and down against me. Unfortunately, when the day came to film, although tethered by the nose and still as affectionate as before, the bull was equally determined not to stand still. The scene required that it should, but there was no arguing with it. Sorry not to be able to use such a splendid creature, we reluctantly had to move on.

It was interesting to watch Jack being paid by his clients. In *All Creatures Great and Small* we had sequences where the locals would turn up and push what they owed across the desk to Siegfried. Some were reluctant, some were grateful, and others paid only the amount they could afford. But always in cash. So it was with Jack some forty years later. Unlike most of the transactions today, where the shopkeeper carefully counts through the money you have just counted out to him, Jack never checked the large sums of money that would be given over to him. If a man said it was £59 as he thrust a pile of notes forward, then £59 it was. 'Anything off for luck?' was the constant request. Jack would peel off a fiver. Knowing the Herriot books are set in earlier times, it was reassuring to find that there were still some values that remained the same.

Perhaps it was fortunate that on my last morning about the Watkinson practice, as Jack and I were motoring along a country lane, a farmer flagged us down.

'My dog here whose paw you stitched up the other day. Do you want to take out the stitches now or shall I bring him to the surgery?' he asked.

'I'll do it now,' said Jack. He placed the dog on the bonnet of his Range Rover and removed the stitches with a knife from his kit-bag.

In payment the farmer gave us a flagon of homemade beer which he had fetched from the house. We sat on the grassy roadside to drink it. Not a car passed down the lane. Not a movement broke the stillness of the hazy green Yorkshire landscape as it undulated beneath the clear blue sky. It was perfect. You could have been back in the time of Herriot's books. Only the sleek fawn car drawn up alongside reminded me that indeed I was in the 1970s.

*

When my week with the Watkinsons all too swiftly came to an end, I was very sad. With the casting aside of my London clothes, and the dark glasses which had never sat comfortably on my face in the first place, I had discovered a whole new way of life which totally engrossed me.

chapter five

That weekend Terry Dudley came up to Yorkshire. Collecting me from the Watkinson's, we had a final couple of days checking over the locations where we would start filming on the Monday.

As we drove away he told me that Robert Hardy should have been with him. The terrible irony was that Robert's daughter had the day before been severely injured in a riding accident. She was on the danger list. Subdued and nervous for them both, we passed an anxious twenty-four hours. In time to start the filming, Robert was with us. Much to our great relief his daughter had pulled through the danger period. Although she was still very ill, there was every reason to be optimistic.

Robert Hardy asked me how I'd got on. I was able to say that in general I had been all right with animals, but that I was still very wary of horses. I felt horses to be dodgy. Robert Hardy is a first-rate horseman. When called upon as an actor to ride, he tries to use his own highly bred mare. In *Edward VII* as Prince Albert, the horse he rode was his own. With all his vast experience of horses he told me I was very right to be wary. I would be safe as long as I remained that way.

Finally the day arrived. Early on Monday morning we were out on a farm to begin the shoot. I think we were all rather nervous. I know I certainly was. At last I stood there be-costumed, hair newly trimmed, while a battalion of arc lamps threw their strange artificial glare into the morning's light. The camera was set up on its mounts, and seemingly dozens of strange people hovered or scurried around.

'Here goes,' I thought as a make-up girl gave a final dab to my face.

The first shot was of Siegfried and James Herriot walking up a path to a farm building. As the camera rolled and the director called 'Action' we were off. All sorts of things raced through my mind. Must keep the mind blank, I thought. But, instead of it going blank, all the stories I had ever read about actors keeping their minds blank rushed into it. The Hollywood actor who, leaning over a fence, had to gaze at his young daughter as she played on the lawn before him. In the story she was dying of leukaemia and the camera came in close on the anguished face of the actor. 'That was great,' yelled the director when the shot was over, 'what were you thinking of?' he asked. 'I wasn't thinking o' nothin',' came the reply. I remembered too Greta Garbo in *Queen Christina*. In the final shot of the film, as she stands at the bow of a ship, the wind blowing back her hair, the camera comes in close and holds on her unblinking face for what seems like for ever. She has just abdicated from her throne for the sake of the man she loves who, moments before, has died in her arms. There is not much you can say after that, but a lot of things might be running through your mind. The director told her not to think of anything. The large limpid eyes in her expressionless face would say more than any words or expression could . . .

I don't know what I was expecting. All I had to do was walk up a path with Robert Hardy. I was only aware that I was at the threshold of big things.

Years before, when I had been at the National Theatre, a pause in rehearsal had brought me up beside Maggie Smith. It must have been my first season in such august company. I was just one of half a dozen eager young actors who understudied and played walk-ons. As yet I had hardly dared speak to those eminent actors topped by Laurence Olivier who headed the cast. Although it was a wonderful company none of whom were conscious of hierarchy, we, fresh in at the bottom of it, had not yet begun to relax, and I don't suppose those at the top had yet sorted out which of us was which. Searching about for a conversational gambit and anxious to appear friendly, Maggie Smith asked me what I wanted from my career. Wanting a lot from it, jokingly I said something which was a bit truer that I intended: 'I want to walk on stage and have all the ladies swoon at my good looks.' Maggie Smith just looked at me in the way that has since won her Oscars.

Wanting to cut a dashing figure I have been rather pulled up short by what nature has given me. Instead of the girls swooning it is their mums that go, 'Ah! Isn't he nice!' There must be something homely and reassuring about the image I project.

Filming for an episode of *Van der Valk*, the successful drama series set in Holland, as the cast got together for initial rehearsals, the director brought the make-up girl over to me. 'Now, Chris here plays a barman. I want him to look very dishy.' The make-up girl remained silent, shaking her head in disbelief. She may have been called upon to do some strange things in her time, but never had she had to go this far. In the event, she peroxided my mid-brown hair to white blond. It looked wonderful for the television camera and almost had the effect the director intended. Outside in the daylight it was quite another matter. It looked dreadfully phoney. I had a hard time of it just trying to walk down the street. Every couple of yards I would be stopped by strange people wanting a light. When I proffered the match, my hand would be held a fraction too long!

It must have been the boy-next-door quality that made me right for James Herriot. As the make-up girl trimmed down my hair on that first morning, she must have been reassured to see that only a slight modification was required. Never minding having short hair, I was quite happy for her to snip away. I know too short a short-back-and-sides does look odd today, but it gives me the horrors when I hear of actors who have turned down parts for fear of a haircut. The job has to come first.

For the film *Virgin Soldiers*, playing a 1950s private, surely the ultimate in short hair, I had rushed to a local barber in Essex, where we were living at the time. 'A short back and sides,' I cried as I settled in the chair. The barber, an old man, could not believe his luck. He fumbled and shook, repeatedly asking me if he had heard correctly, and in ecstasy set to with the scissors.

Arriving at Singapore airport with a number of other young actors all of whom were to play soldiers, we were greeted by the film's director, John Dexter. Pulling me from the huddled ranks of travel-weary players all of whom had been to fashionable London hairdressers who had given them careful hair-styles, he pointed at my sort of turnip-top. 'This is how you are going to have to get your hair cut,' he said, and frogmarched them off to the barber.

It was because of a haircut that John Dexter became god-father to my second child, Nicholas, now aged twelve. John Dexter is without doubt one of the handful of top-rung theatre directors in the world. A brilliant man, he gave to the National Theatre some of its finest productions before being appointed to the New York Metropolitan Opera House, where he is now. A man noted for his stringency and his ability to leave most actors quaking in their shoes, I was no exception. But, for some reason, throughout the early days of my career he was my mentor. Having worked with us a little at drama school, he gave me my first job when I left. In a small part and understudying, I went with the English Stage Company to New York to present *Chips With Everything*. I was there for five months and had a most wonderful time. 'Well, if nothing else, it will give you a holiday,' said John when I rushed up to shower him profusely with thanks.

Walking about on that first day of arrival in New York I could not believe it. The policemen all leant against walls chewing gum with hands resting on guns at the hip; even the telephones were just like I'd seen in the movies. Above all, the taxi cabs were yellow! Being pre-Beatle – New York was in fact filling up with advance publicity for their imminent arrival – a short haircut was quite normal and in no way impeded my social life.

It was John Dexter too who upon my return from America extricated me from the Worthing Repertory Company where I was working, and invited me to join the National Theatre for his production of *Royal Hunt of the Sun*. The newly formed National Theatre Company was at the time performing down at Chichester. The season consisted of three plays, *Royal Hunt* with Colin Blakely and Robert Stephens, *Othello* with Laurence Olivier and Maggie Smith, and a Restoration piece with amongst others Billie Whitelaw in the lead. I appeared only in *Royal Hunt*.

The season over, I was asked to join the company on a year's contract when they moved to the Old Vic in London. I would be in all the productions. In *Othello* John Dexter gave me the part of Second Gent. There was a speech which had been cut at Chichester, but was now given to me. It contained one of the most difficult lines I have ever had to say: '*I never did like molestation view On the enchafed flood.*' The words are ingrained on my mind: John Dexter took me over them again and again. When the line had been spoken down at Chichester, the voice of Olivier had clipped from the stalls, 'No. Nor no rose garden either!' – which was presumably why it was cut.

The first thing I was to do on my entrance in this scene was to point with my arm outstretched. There I was in front of an audience on the stage of the Old Vic, a legendary place. I couldn't believe it! I was so frightened that the wide-flung gesture I had rehearsed became a shrivelled-up little wave of the finger. Afterwards John Dexter just shook his head and raised his eyes to the ceiling.

It was a year or so later when he came up to me in the bar where I stood with a number of fellow actors. Sue was pregnant at the time, and John was about to direct the Russian play *The Storm*. Despite everything I have said about my willingness to have my hair cut there are limits beyond which it is hard to go. 'Chris,' he said, 'I want you to shave your head.' My mouth must have fallen open in shock. 'Or let me be godfather to your next child.'

So it was not so much the haircut which worried the make-up girl that first day on *All Creatures Great and Small*. It was more the colour.

Throughout my career my hair has gone from blond to dark brown and back again in accordance with whatever the script required. I had already gone blond for *Van der Valk* when shortly afterwards I did the Young Vic production of *Rosencrantz and Guildenstern are Dead*. Because Richard O'Callaghan, who played opposite me, was very dark it seemed good contrast for me

67

to remain blond. Soon after that came *Murder Most English*. There again, Anton Rodgers is dark and so, as his side-kick, I remained blond. Soon after that came *All Creatures*. With the weeks before starting filled with work, the blond had no chance of growing out. When the wife of the real James Herriot was first told who would be playing the Herriot character, her comment was, 'Oh . . . not that boy with the awful-coloured hair.'

Later, when she told me that that had been her reaction, she must have caught me when I was a bit fraught, for I crisply replied, 'Then there must be something wrong with your set!' Maybe my scalp was feeling a bit sore.

It was because of my hair that my initial meeting with James Herriot himself was not as momentous as it should have been.

Within a day or two the dye the make-up girl had used to turn me from blond back to dark had faded in the sunlight to a rather startling orange. Giving up on permanent dyes, she had decided to merely rinse my hair brown at the beginning of every day until the blond had finally grown out. It looked fine as long as it didn't rain. Then dark rivulets would trickle down my face. To counteract this I was given a fold-up plastic hood of the type you see scurrying up and down the high street whenever it rains. As I stood waiting between shots in my plastic bonnet and tweeds I did not present a very prepossessing figure.

At the meeting in London when we in the cast met each other for the first time, Robert Hardy and I expressed an obvious wish to meet the real James Herriot. We were told that we must wait, eventually we would, but though he enjoyed the success of his books, his primary concern was his veterinary practice. He was a quiet, retiring man, we were informed. With all the resultant publicity surrounding his books, he had become even more anxious to be left in peace.

One drizzly day, filming in a backstreet of a village some two weeks after starting, as I stood between takes with Robert Hardy deliberating on the script and looking as fetching as ever in my plastic bonnet, there was a tap on my shoulder. 'Are you Christopher Timothy?' asked a soft Scottish voice.

'Yes, yes I am,' I answered a bit abruptly, trying to imply I did not wish to be disturbed as I really had to talk with Robert Hardy about the work in hand.

'I am your alter ego,' said the voice.

My blood ran cold. I turned round and there facing me was the man himself.

He is truly delightful. As far as I can see he has only one flaw: the measure of whisky he pours you is too generous! At a quiet dinner that James Herriot, Carol Drinkwater, Peter Davison and I had at his home, the whisky and soda he gave me was so strong I had to go and help his wife in the kitchen for fear of being given another and falling in a stupor on the floor.

On another evening a large dinner party was arranged. It was for all those concerned with the filming and for the real-life Herriots and Siegfried Farnon. Unfortunately both Peter Davison and myself missed it as we were out night-filming, but I was told that it had been a great evening. Apparently Mrs Herriot had brought with her a photograph of herself as a young woman which nobody had seen. The resemblance between the girl in the photo and Carol was extraordinary. The more so because when Carol was cast for the part there had been no consideration of whether she looked like the person she portrayed or not.

Meeting the Herriots on a number of occasions and realizing what lovely people they were, both Robert Hardy and I agreed as soon as we knew we had the jobs, we should have jumped in the car and driven up to meet them.

Driving to Yorkshire one time with Robert Hardy, we decided we would call in on the real Siegfried Farnon. Having missed the dinner party I had yet to meet him.

We arrived at a beautiful house set in a bowl in the landscape. No one was at home, so after walking around a bit and waiting, with still no sign of anyone, we reluctantly decided that we would have to drive on. Just as we were climbing back into the car, up he drove.

We were urged to stay for tea and then shown about the house.

He had with him a number of dogs. As we left every room he would call, 'Come on dogs,' in exactly the way I had seen Robert Hardy do countless times in the studio. It gave me an extraordinary sensation of having been there before.

In the studio the pack of dogs you see around Skeldale House is comprised of the pair of labradors belonging to the producer Bill Sellars, the sheep dog of the script editor Ted Rhodes, the chow of the production unit manager John Nathan Turner, and the whippet, Christy, which belongs to Robert Hardy.

All lovely dogs as they may be, they are the devil to work with. Not being trained for the studio, they ramble around constantly wandering off the set just at the moment they are needed. It is difficult to herd them together and keep them in one place. The rooms at 'Skeldale' are built for camera mobility and usually only have two, sometimes three walls. Definitely not the four with a solid door you need for that bunch.

Bill Sellars says that when he is watching *All Creatures* at home on television and Robert Hardy as Siegfried calls, 'Come on dogs,' his labradors jump to their feet and head expectantly to the door.

Robert Hardy declares that his whippet, Christy, is his worst critic! As he is acting away as Siegfried with Christy also in the scene, the dog looks at him, a kind of 'must he?' expression on his face, and then turns away in embarrassment.

Needing to telephone James Herriot but having mislaid the number, I called Robert Hardy to ask him for it. He said he didn't have it either, but if I called Siegfried he would tell me, and he gave me the number. Speaking to the real Siegfried a moment later, I thought I had made a mistake and dialled Robert Hardy again. The voices were identical.

With barely a ripple in the quiet Yorkshire landscape we were able to begin filming. Obviously the farmers on whose land we were would come to watch. Maybe a friend or two would also be with them. In the villages only those whose peace was suddenly disturbed by the blaze of the arc lamps and the hubbub of two dozen people would venture from their houses to have a look. Often the people whose houses or land we were using had known the real James Herriot. They knew as well, despite the steps he had taken to disguise the characters in the books, just who he was writing about. It gave them great enjoyment when someone was depicted as being mean or was shown in any other light than the one the person wanted to be seen in. Often the characters were still alive, the locals pointing out the real people with glee. Mrs Pumphrey of Tricki Woo fame was still alive, we were told, and greatly enjoyed seeing herself 'immortalized' in Margaretta Scott's wonderful performance.

It was difficult to find a pekinese quite as pampered and obese as Tricki Woo, an animal that looked as though it might suffer from 'flop-bot' and 'cracker-dog'. In the event, the pekinese we used was a very healthy little dog whose fur was heavily backcombed to make him look twice the size.

James Herriot said his stories were ninety-nine per cent true; the only 'poetic licence' he had taken was in switching the time around. An incident that occurred in the 1949s or 50s he would set in the 1930s.

As the filming progressed more people would hear about it and come to watch. After the first series had started to run on television and became the extraordinary success it did, large crowds of tourists as well as locals would gather to watch as we worked. Nearly always attentive and responsive, they took to being shoved around so as not to intrude 'in shot' with great good humour.

The most frequent request to them was, 'Would you please be careful not to laugh.' The noise of up to two hundred people enjoying their day out would sometimes quite destroy the sound recording, and we would have to do it again, stretching was what already a tightly packed schedule.

I enjoyed it enormously, as I think we all did. Although we had to work very hard and fast, sometimes becoming a bit tetchy when things went repeatedly wrong and time not allowing us to get it right, it was great fun. We were lucky that everybody connected with it seemed to get on with only the occasional jarring note – a rare thing when a couple of dozen 'artistic' tempera-ments are gathered together. The spirit of cooperation was strong, presided over by the enigmatic Bill Sellars, who kept a watchful eye that the tone of the series should never become over-comic or unnecessarily gloomy. I think in particular of the sequence when I had to wear a rubber calving suit.

This was not filmed in the first six weeks of summer shooting, but as 'strike' filming one day in November. It was freezing cold and we filmed in a derelict farm building that was part of an army firing-range. There wasn't a wall standing that was not riddled with holes, giving us about as much protection from the icy wind as a cheese-grater. Because of the nature of my costume, which was more like cast iron than rubber, I could only just wear a pair of underpants underneath. My nose was purple with cold and my ears had long since packed up. I thought I would die!

This sequence was considered rather dodgy to do. James Herriot was to be made a fool of. When it went out a lot of people didn't like it for that reason. The point was, though, that James Herriot was not some kind of infallible 'super-hero'. He was intensely human. At the time he was new to the practice, nervous and shy. But with the scene's farcical overtones we were all a bit wary of it. One of the directors had refused to do it point blank. Bill Sellars believed it could be made to work, and in the end Terry Dudley directed it with great restraint, making it very funny without slipping into farce. Cryptic notes would be passed to me: 'Ask Chris to be careful in that shot,' and 'Don't let Chris go over the top.'

We were lucky too with our directors. Highly skilled, they were all extremely sympathetic to work with. Peter Moffatt with his wife Joan Kemp-Welch, a director with whom I have done a couple of plays, both came to see me in *Rosencrantz and Guilden-stern*. Having met him, it was good to work with him. He was particularly clever at getting first-rate performances from the children who appeared in various episodes. I suppose most adult actors are kids at heart, needing constantly to be given reassurance and a congratulatory pat on the head in the way kids do.

Robert Tronson at first worried me a bit. A deeply thoughtful man, he would pace slowly about the set ruminating. At the end of each shot, if he liked what we had done he would say, 'Mmmm ... very good,' but in such a way that I would instantly panic.' He doesn't like it,' I'd think. He was not a man to waste words. It was a few days before I learnt to accept his judgement implicitly and realize what a special director he is.

It seems unfair to single out names, for each of the directors brought to *All Creatures* an approach that was his own and which, when the episodes combined, added up to a complete picture. That of course is the art of the producer, whose skill it is to select the directors, writers and cast who will best serve the finished product. With the subject matter we had for *All Creatures Great and Small* the BBC was on to a winner from the start. But it could easily not have been as successful as it was. Reaching number one in the viewing figures, an unheard-of accolade for a drama series, it swept the board with the awards it won.

Each of the directors wanted to be the first, for then it would be they who helped to mould the characters we played. This was especially so with the relationship between Helen Alderson and James Herriot. A good old-fashioned love story, it was not until episode seven that we were married. Each director in turn built up the picture and pushed the characters along, helping us to grow and expand within them, adding greater depth to the story-line.

Robert Hardy was an instrumental force behind us younger actors. In those first few weeks when we were a bit keyed-up he helped us to relax. He would watch us all the time as we worked. If he saw we were a bit flummoxed by something we were doing he would offer us constructive advice put in such a way it could only be helpful. For one actor to advise another is usually a pretty risky business, however well meant and however much the other actor needs the help. The actor floundering around tends to take any advice offered except by the director as an insult to his abilities. The more insecure he is feeling the more self-protective he becomes.

The writing of the episodes was first rate, done by a number of writers. Always pleased to be able to give young writers a chance, Bill Sellars made certain that the scripts were up to scratch. Occasionally in rehearsal, though, we would have some trouble trying to get the mood of a scene. Maybe a line jarred, creating a problem, or something said by a character didn't ring true. Robert Hardy would at such times say, 'Back to the book,' instantly producing the Herriot book from which the story in question had been adapted. There was none of this 'Now let me see. I know it's in here somewhere,' followed by a half-hour flick through the pages broken only by an apologetic 'I'm certain I saw it, you know,' as the rummage continued. Robert's books were all neatly cross-referenced with the scripts; stick-out labels indexed almost every line. Within a split-second the book was open at the appropriate page. Within moments the offending line was altered and rehearsals progressed.

Because of the horrible equation 'time costs money', as I have said, of necessity we worked to a very tight schedule. When filming there was very little time to turn round: from the word 'action', time dictated you got it right. This was true in the studio as well. As the clock approached ten p.m. on the second of the two days allotted for the recording of each episode, the production team would get a bit tetchy. To run past ten o'clock and go into overtime cost the earth, and though you and the technical staff were always hopeful, as the minutes ticked up to the witching hour things would be made to move at a hell of a lick to get them all in.

In front of the camera, either filming on location or in the studio, any amount of things can go wrong. There is that technical expression probably unintelligible to the newcomer which makes you feel so clued in when you authoritatively bandy it about in answer to someone else's hesitant 'What's wrong?' 'Oh. There's a hair in the gate,' you airily reply with a shrug of your shoulders. Particularly appropriate when, to the untutored observer of the making of *All Creatures Great and Small*, it might have a more literal meaning, a 'hair in the gate' is exactly that. A bit of fluff may be caught in the camera lens, spoiling the picture. Perhaps a plane has flown over at an inappropriate moment, or a car engine has revved up in the background. Even the set may have fallen down without you realizing. Often, though, it is your fault. You have got a line back to front or perhaps the prop you were operating has repeatedly failed to function. Whatever it is that has gone wrong, be it your fault or not, the general feeling of persecution a young actor has makes him automatically suspect it must be he who is responsible for the hold-up in valuable time.

On the studio floor around you are official-looking people wearing headphones. On these they receive messages from the powers in the control gallery, the director and producer. These people with the 'cans', to you with your natural inferiority complex, definitely have that sense of 'belonging', of being 'in the know'. When, because of some fault or technical hitch, everything grinds to a halt, you can just discern a sort of irate high-pitched jabber from the 'cans' of the person standing next to you. You have a strong sensation that the skies have parted and God is pointing a finger at you. You pray it might be somebody or something else. But no. The man with the earphones, as he listens to the stream of four-letter words issuing from them, has turned his thoughtful gaze on you. The jangling stops; he comes over to you. 'Chris love, the director says, it's smashing but do you think you could say the line as we rehearsed it?' And he wanders off with a smile. 'Ready to go again,' he calls.

There are many times when from the actor's point of view a shot has not been right. Perhaps he feels he has not been able to give proper weight to the words, or the mood has eluded him. To everybody else it seems perfectly good, but the actor knows it could be better. To humour the distinguished actor the director will often do the shot again, but the young actor has to be very upset before that will happen. Robert Hardy had the knack and the authority for the shot to be repeated. Carol, Peter Davison and myself, however much we protested, just had to make do. I

75

remember a scene involving the three of us that would not go right. Of course it looked fine to everybody else. It is the only time I have ever seen Peter lose his cool. Although, certainly in the early days, he was often nervous, he is generally the most equable, even-tempered bloke. This time he dashed his cigarette to the floor and jumped up and down on it swearing volubly Needless to say, even this had no effect. I was so amazed by this vision, I forgot my own consternation.

When in scenes with Robert Hardy we had to laugh, it was always genuine. His antics as Siegfried would have us rolling on the floor. At times when we had to remain straight-faced it made things a bit difficult.

There was a sequence when Tristan and James, having wheedled away at Siegfried, finally persuaded him to lend us his car. Of course we instantly pranged it. Swerving to avoid a huddle of sheep, Tristan scraped it along a wall. The accident itself was faked. Whereas it looked as though it was happening, in fact we were touching nothing at all. We might as well have done, for the prop-man then removed the car doors and laid them on the ground. Peter and I spent a very satisfying half-hour giving vent to our latent hooliganism. Hitting them with bricks and jumping up and down, we beat the living daylights out of them. But James and Tristan then had to report back to Siegfried. He was lying in bed pretending to be ill. 'Come closer, I can't hear you,' he kept saying to the nervous Tristan who reluctantly edged the while across the room towards him. When Tristan was almost on top of him, abandoning his sick-bed, Siegfried leapt up yelling at him and grabbed his lapels.

The way Robert Hardy did it was so funny it took many takes before we could do it properly, acting fear instead of being incapacitated with laughter.

chapter six

It was another beautiful summer's day. We had broken for lunch. Taking our plates of food from the caterer's truck, we pottered about shirtless trying to catch the sun. Replete, we lay back enjoying our regulation one hour off. We chattered idly and perhaps deliberated on the afternoon's work that stretched ahead of us. An opportune moment for Johnny Pearson, the composer of the theme music, to arrive. Taking a cassette player from his car, he set it on the bonnet and played to us the theme music for *All Creatures* he had just composed. Johnny wrote the theme music for *Owen MD* which became a popular hit. Unplanned, his arrival at the location could not have been better timed. The music, as it wafted through the still summer's air, seemed perfectly to catch the mood of the Yorkshire moors stretching around us, and the spirit of the stories in which we were involved.

An actor friend, who had worked with me both at Farnham where I had recently played Petruchio in *The Taming of the Shrew* and later as the farmer in the rubber-suit sequence I have described, told me that when on Sundays he and his young daughter ride horseback down Box Hill, a steep incline in the countryside south of London, his daughter would demand that, starting at the top and not stopping until they reach the bottom, he hum this theme music, while she is the laughing James Herriot as in the opening sequences of the series every week.

Often people ask me what we were laughing at when the camera shows close-ups of our faces in the opening credits. I'm afraid it was nothing to do with *All Creatures Great and Small*. Knowing there was no sound recording, for there would be the theme music playing, someone had just said something rude. As much as I would like to set it down it is unprintable. But at the time it was very funny.

The car you also see in those opening credits zooming along over the moors looked wonderful and was lovely to drive. Enjoying it enormously, I was only too happy to zip around in it. Had I known!

There was a sequence when James Herriot, in pursuit of Helen, goes to her farm on the pretext of checking a calf's broken leg. His courtship does not go all that smoothly. Nervous as he is, things have a habit of not turning out as he anticipates. In the first place he had rushed out with his coat flung over his pyjamas. Stepping from the car to greet Helen, his coat catches in the door, revealing his pyjamas underneath. Not the romantic figure he wanted to present. His treatment of the calf done, and watched by Helen with an amused glint in her eye, increasingly fumblingly he climbs back into the car. Where James was parked in the front of the Alderson home is a circular courtyard. Looking at Helen, James drives round the courtyard and out. Unfortunately, as I turned from looking at Carol I saw the car did not have the space in which to complete its turn. It was about to hit the wall. I slammed on the brakes, but on full lock they didn't operate. With a crunch the car collided with the wall. Instead of just reversing and driving on, giving a final funny twist to James's agitated meeting, I swore loudly and jumped from the car. 'Cut!' the director had to shout, and we filmed it again, this time without mishap.

If I had known at the time of filming the credits that with any slight swerve the car had no brakes, I certainly would not have enjoyed it. I wouldn't even have gone near the car in the first place.

One of the most constructive things they could have taught us at school would have been how to drive. But of course they didn't. Sue and I have always chosen to live outside London. At times this has necessitated some hard travelling, primarily because Sue loves the country. Later, when our family began to grow, the country seemed a much better place to bring up the kids. Other than those short periods when as a child I lived briefly at my grandparents' flat in Kensington, and for my three years at drama school, I have never lived in London itself.

When first I went to the Central School of Speech and Drama I stayed in a bedsitter near to the school. It was one of those large London houses with every room divided up, giving the landlady maximum income from minimal space. The building was probably condemned a long time ago. I loved it. It seemed to me what struggling in the theatre was all about. I had a small metal bed and a gas-ring with a meter attached. The gas-ring was for both heating the room and cooking on. I was at the top of a long flight of stairs. The rent was £2 a week, and if you wanted a bath, it was extra. My mother, in a visit down from Shrewsbury, was horrified. It seemed very romantic to me. However, I had no peace until I moved to a flat in Golders Green. My mother, selling her house in Shrewsbury and looking for somewhere nearer to London, promptly came to stay.

All my life money had been tight. Helpful as my grandparents were, my mother had quite a battle to support both Jon and me. Before I had properly finished at the private prep school I was at the cash flow gave out. Moving to Shrewsbury I was sent to the grammar school. My mother worked at a series of jobs, mostly teaching needlework. For a time, on one of our brief spells in London, my mother taught sewing to a group of prostitutes in Soho. I'm a bit hazy about the details now and I'm certain it was thought unsuitable to explain them to me then, seven years old as I was. I do remember accompanying her though on a number of occasions. My most distinct memory was of the radio programme with Valentine Dyall, *The Man in Black*. As with most of the nation, everything ground to a halt whilst, for half an hour, we were riveted.

Another incident at about this period I have never quite fathomed either. 'We are going to see a doctor-man,' my mother informed me as we stood by the bus-stop one day. The trouble was, I had an unfortunate habit of stealing money. My mother and grandmother were forever discovering they had less in their purses than they thought they had. I would be up at the local cinema watching the children's matinée with my mates when a small calculation showed that my pocket money had expired a day or so before. The cleaner would be paid and on going to her handbag she'd discover there was nothing in it. I would be sitting on the hearth-rug playing with a new toy that only minutes before I didn't have.

'He is very nice and is just going to ask you a few questions,' my mother reassured me as we walked into the hospital, and left me in a room with an elderly grey-haired man in a white coat.

'Now Christopher, tell me about some of the naughty things you do.'

'Well . . . sometimes I'm not very nice to my brother Jon,' I piped up, thinking of the time when my mother had snatched a carving knife from my hands as I declared, 'I'm going to go out and cut Jon's head off.'

'And what else?' asked the man.

'I sometimes say I've had one biscuit when I've really had two,' I offered helpfully.

'Yes. And what else?' he went on.

Goodness! This was harder than I thought. What strange things grown-ups wanted to know. I racked my brains.

'Yesterday I was rude to Granny,' I chirped, glad to have been able to think of something. 'And when I say I've cleaned my teeth I haven't.' It was all coming now in a rush.

'Very good. What else?'

'I . . . er . . .' I stammered eagerly, beginning to like this game, and then couldn't think of anything to say. I had learnt at school that when we were dead God would ask us questions just like this. Perhaps this was a test-run.

'You can't think of anything else?' he prompted.

'No,' I said puzzled. Was there something awful about me he knew and I didn't? 'No,' I repeated doubtfully.

'Well, Christopher, you steal money, don't you?' He leant towards me.

'Oh *that*,' I said, relieved. Was that all he was on about?

'Tell me why you think you steal the money.'

The house where I was born. 'Tan Rhiw', Bala, Wales.

My parents and I at my christening.

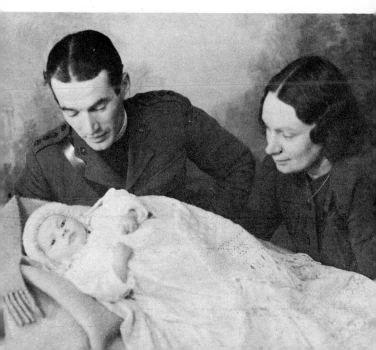

(above) Jon and I in 1947. Jon's the one with his tongue hanging out.

(below) Dress rehearsal for the Wheatsheaf Players production of *Strictly Business*, May 1960. Guess which one is me!

(opposite above left) Sue and the kids. Clockwise from the top left-hand corner: Simon, Tabitha, Nicholas, Robin, David, Kate and Sue in the middle. (©Syndication International)

(opposite above right) Doing a bit of publicity with Sue for *The Virgin Soldiers* at the Odeon Harlow, Essex.

(opposite below left) As Toulouse-Lautrec for the *Sun* commercial.

(opposite below right) As Sidney H. Fox – hanged for matricide in the Thames TV production of *Killers*. (©Thames Television)

(above) As Petruchio in *The Taming of the Shrew*, with Charlotte Cornwell as Kate. The Redgrave Theatre, Farnham.

(left) With Anton Rodgers in *Murder Most English*. (© BBC)

(opposite above) John Kenway risking life and limb. I just sit there!

(opposite below) Yet *another* meal round that table: Tristan (Peter Davison), Helen (Carol Drinkwater), Mrs Hall (Mary Hignett) and me as James Herriot. (© BBC)

(left) Robert Hardy. (© BBC)

(right) With the white coats in the surgery. Note the varying sizes! (© BBC)

(opposite) Taking a break during shooting! The only time you'll ever see this James Herriot in a hat. (© BBC)

(below) Here we go again! *'. . . I don't know, Siegfried.'* (© BBC)

(left) Peter and I in the battle for Boris the cat. (© BBC)

(right) Carol and I on the Yorkshire moors. (© BBC)

(below) The book just would not be complete without a picture of Tricki Woo. And of course the delectable Mrs Pumphrey (Margaretta Scott). (© BBC)

''Cos if I've got the money I can go to the cinema and I can go into shops and buy toys,' I answered reasonably.

'Oh!' He seemed rather taken aback by my logic. Perhaps he had expected me to say the reasons he later told my mother. 'Christopher feels subconsciously he is not getting the love and attention he needs. As a substitute he takes the money.'

When I think of my childhood, the one thing we were never short of was love! I wanted the money for exactly the reasons I told him. As soon as it was pointed out to me how wrong it was, then I stopped. It had just been one of the passing phases any child goes through. In my teenage years my mother might have needed a bit of help, but then it was James Dean and Elvis Presley who should have taken the blame! Even twenty years later as I walked about as James Herriot it was their influence I had to be careful of. As a would-be teddy-boy I had developed a kind of rolling gait. So ingrained in me did it become that, unless I literally watched my step, it reappeared. Something that went down well with my mates in Shrewsbury was definitely not going to reassure the good people of Darrowby, or win me the hand of Helen Alderson, who already found James Herriot amusing enough.

When I got to drama school everything I did was in imitation of James Dean. It must have clashed terribly with the more classical elements of English Drama.

'For Heaven's sake! Forget about James Dean,' an irate director shouted at me one day as I picked my nose and mumbled through one of Shakespeare's nobler speeches. 'If you must think of anyone, then let it be Montgomery Clift!' A meticulous and brilliant screen actor, I should have thought of him before. Too late to undo the damage done to my movement. It certainly clarified my mind.

Having won a place at drama school, the Shropshire County Council said no to my request for a grant. So the drama school gave me the John Gielgud Scholarship, which paid the fees for my first term and gave me £2 a week to spend. To help support myself I took a job in a nearby transport café. I would go early in the morning to help at breakfast time, rush back at lunch, and do a bit of washing-up in the evenings. On top of my wages I was also allowed to eat free of charge.

It sounds ideal but the big draw-back was I stank all day long of fried eggs, bacon and chips. The girls in my class would ask not to play love scenes with me. Even the girl I struck up an uneasy relationship with, Star Anchor-Simmons, must have had second thoughts. A beautiful girl with an equally striking name, she soon became homesick, returning to her horses and the country-side.

Perhaps because of this early deprivation, I have always liked love scenes. Only infrequently have I played them. With this current fashion for making obvious emotions obscure, I can't think of anything nicer to say than, 'I love you. I love you.' If violins strike up and roses come into bloom then even better.

I thought the directors on *All Creatures Great and Small* handled the courtship of James and Helen beautifully. It was a delight to do. Carol Drinkwater, although I sometimes found her methods of work at variance with my own, was wonderful as Helen. I know I'm not biased when I say that. I know too there has been a great deal of sensationalized journalism surrounding our private lives, but throughout the several months it took to make the first series, we were never more than colleagues. By the time our relationship developed, we were well into the second series. That was a good year after we first started working together. By then a great deal had happened in my own life that had nothing to do with Carol. My wife Sue and Carol are good friends. Whatever the newspapers say, they both know the very ordinary facts.

For some reason I forget now, after the first term at drama school I qualified for a grant from the London County Council. I went along to audition for nine or ten severe-looking people all of whom I distinctly felt would have been more at home in an accounts department rather than discerning the potential skill of a would-be actor. The disapproval was mutual. With an assumed Welsh accent I gave them a bit of Danny in *Night Must*

Fall, a part I had played as an amateur. When I had finished they looked at each other. 'What other accents can you do?' asked one, and prepared to write down a list.

'Well. I can do a North Country and I can do a Cockney one,' I answered.

'Oh yes. Any others?' and he held the pencil poised over the still empty sheet of paper.

With all the scorn of a first-year drama student I wanted to say of what secondary importance an accent was to an actor. It's got nothing to do with the art of acting, I wanted to say. If an actor needs to use an accent he goes out and learns one and then gets on with the major job of making the character live.

I didn't. I just said, 'No,' humbly.

'Well, that's not very good,' I could hear them thinking.

After a silence one of them asked me, 'And what academic qualifications do you have?'

Perhaps because I was fairly certain my count of one O-level was not at that point going to impress them, or maybe because my student scorn had by that time reached such a pitch, I patronizingly replied, 'I don't think my academic qualifications have anything to do with it.'

They must have bristled at this, for the next question was, 'What will you do if we don't give you the grant?'

I hadn't been at drama school for nothing. With erect carriage, my head thrown back, and in my best newly acquired tones, I flung at them, 'I shan't leave drama school, because I'm going to be an actor. If you don't give me the money then I'll find some other way of getting it.'

After that there was not much any of us could say. The interview ended. It must have been the last of the stands I had to make in order to become an actor, and the first of the much harder battles to succeed.

Afterwards, on my return to Central, John Blatchley, the principal of the school who, along with his colleagues Yat Malgram and Christopher Fettis, has helped to shape several generations of British actors, asked me how I got on.

'I don't think they'll give it to me,' I said despondently.

'That will be a pity,' he replied, disappearing into his office and leaving me glum-faced in the corridor.

Although nothing has ever been said, I am certain now he straightaway telephoned the board and recommended I be given the grant – an act for which I am eternally grateful.

It was whilst at drama school that I performed in my first film. The storyline often comes to mind, making me laugh at inappropriate moments. Life must have been more black and white in those days. I was working at Sainsbury's to supplement my grant when a friend asked me to help make a short film to enter for his amateur movie-makers club award. The story I worked out was a boy-meets-girl. The young man arrives in London and meets a girl. He makes a pass at her and she promptly faints. He panics and runs away to stand by a river, debating whether or not to throw himself in. A kindly passer-by, played by an uncle of Sue's, takes the boy home and gives him a cup of coffee. Fortified, he goes back to the girl and everything is all right. There was no sound. Later, using an old tape recorder, we gave it a documentary-sound backing track. Clutching my guitar and playing the only song I knew, 'Tuti-Fruti' I talked over the action, helping to make clear the anguish everyone was going through. Later, when it was known that people actually liked it, we re-recorded it using a guitarist from the pop group I was trying to manage. A disastrous excursion into a field I finally had to admit knowing nothing about, the guitarist certainly knew a few more songs than I did. Amazingly enough the film won the award for best sound track and played for a week at the National Film Theatre along with the other award-winning entries. It got a good response, the notices it received being really quite enthusiastic. Needless to say, it fired off a volley of letters from me. I still had another couple of years to go at drama school. We were strictly banned from working in professional fields until we had finished our training. But it was good practice.

*

I was still practising to drive when I took Sue to hospital to have our first child. Foolhardy I know, but with my work schedule there was nothing else for it. I had bought an old banger from a colleague. In the dawn light Sue would drive me into London and dump me in Holland Park where I would be collected by the fight arranger for the National Theatre who would then take me on to work. Sue would drive back to Essex in time to open up the chemists where she was working. Once when I drove round in a van to drop off some stuff, Sue still in hospital, I was stopped by the local policeman. He asked me to present my driving licence at the Police Station the next day. My test was booked for the next morning. I passed. I rushed round to the police station waving my driving licence with its new pink slip. He looked at it and saw the date. He looked at me through narrowed eyes as I stood before him, hardly daring to breathe. 'All right,' he finally said, closing the licence and handing it back.

When I played Petruchio in *Taming of the Shrew* it was opposite Charlotte Cornwell of *Rock Follies* fame. She played Kate. The theatre was at Farnham in Surrey. Although only a short way home to Godalming where I then lived, the route would have been a very long way round had I taken public transport. A car was indispensable. As I left the theatre late one night I discovered my car would not start. I called up the AA and there was nothing for it but to wait. Working hard to learn my lines, I passed up and down the deserted street. My head buried deeply in the script, I muttered to myself as I went. Preoccupied as I was, I did not notice the mechanic arrive and fix the car. 'OK. Now let's hear your lines,' he said, wiping his hands on a rag as he came up to me. There under a street lamp he heard me through with all the care and precision he had taken to mend the car.

On *All Creatures Great and Small*, frequently needing to drive up to Yorkshire to film or to the studios in Birmingham to record, I decided things would be a lot easier if we were a two-car family. Sue needed our one vehicle for transporting the kids back and forth to school and I had to rely on lifts from other people or go by train. With £300 in cash I went down to our local garage.

'What have you got for this?' I asked the mechanic.

'For that the only car we've got is this Mini,' and he pointed to a cream-coloured object with the front bashed in.

'The engine's very good,' he assured me as I looked a bit doubtful. 'It's got a lot of miles in it yet.'

'I'll take it,' I said.

He was right. It rattled along for a good many months, quite happy to transport me wherever I should wish to go.

Eager to show it off I casually asked my dresser Bill if he would like a lift up to Yorkshire. Of course, with only an hour to go before we were due on location, we got hopelessly lost. Studying the map, having decided down which little lane to go, with time getting exceedingly short, we tore along. The roads on the Yorkshire moors are like a roller-coaster. Going over a hump at great speed we flew through the air in the way you only see in American movies. The car landed with a thud but sped on.

'I better check it's all right,' I gasped, somewhat shaken. I unclipped the safety-belts that had stopped our heads from smashing through the roof with the force of a dozen pile-drivers.

On inspection the car looked all right, but at the point in the middle of the road where we had landed, a large chunk had been gouged from the tarmac. Fragments of concrete lay scattered about. Nothing for it but to rush on, we clambered back into the vehicle. The minute I started up the engine, with a whoosh the heater fell to bits spraying water all over us. For what remained of the journey, Bill had to sit forward holding it together with his knees. He must have regretted ever saying he would come with me. On arrival I was able to find a rock and wedge it under the heater; for the rest of the car's life it was as effective as Bill's knee had been.

Later that afternoon the car's appearance was greatly enhanced by the piece of rope Bill discovered to tie down its bashed-in bonnet.

'I've got a wonderful new car,' said Carol that evening.

'So have I,' I said, not to be outdone.

We rushed outside. There drawn up in front of the hotel were the two cars.

'That's mine,' said Carol with pride, pointing at an enormous Volkswagen Jeep which looked better suited to taking a whole regiment into battle. 'Where's yours?'

'Beside it,' I replied airily, indicating the heap of metal scraped up in the kerb that just about came up to the Jeep's glistening hub caps.

'Oh,' said Carol, lost for words. 'Very nice.'

Bill, my dresser, was ace at coming up with the unexpected. Always attentive, he was a natural in the art of improvisation. There was a sequence when James Herriot, in mock anger at Tristan, has to chase through the woods after him. Tristan crashed through the trees and down a bank. As he went a heavy branch clouted him over the head. It would give a bit more detail, I suggested, if James Herriot, seeing this, decided to be clever and avoid the branch but trip instead. As usual, entering completely into the spirit of the thing, when the director called 'Action,' I hurled myself down the path. A stage fall is a difficult thing to do convincingly. I never quite mastered the art. I succeeded in dodging the branch all right but, momentarily unbalanced, instead of doing a stage fall I genuinely caught my foot in a protruding root and smashed my head into a tree. Although I didn't knock myself out cold, I saw stars. I had to stay lying on the ground. It was fifteen minutes before I had recovered sufficiently to get up and do it again. Meanwhile Bill had produced a cup of hot sweet tea. Goodness knows where he got it from. Filming deep in the woods as we were, we had no location caterers, and the nearest farmhouse must have been miles away.

Although, as an actor, I like to pride myself on the technical skill I have acquired, and never would allow myself to be caught short in the way I was all those years ago, my ability with electrical gadgetry or anything mechanical does, however, still leave a lot to be desired.

It was Peter Davison who with his air of calmness and quiet control would, for example, lean into the engine of my car, fiddle with the appropriate screw and have it running in a trice.

Sheltering from the rain out on location one day, we sat in

Carol's sparkling Jeep. The rain drummed down on the canvas hood above us. We listened to the newly installed cassette machine. Casually I reached out a hand in the general direction of the volume knob. Before I could touch it, the tape snarled up and the machine swung dangling from a wire. 'Oh Goodness! What have I done?' I snapped out of my lethargy. 'Not to *her* machine!' I exclaimed. It being in the middle of the first series our friendship was then merely one of working together. I looked guiltily through the windows to check there was no chance of Carol arriving back from the caravan where she had ducked from the rain. 'What do I tell her?' I asked Peter in desperation. 'It's all right,' he said soothingly, deftly replacing the cassette machine and disengaging the tangle of tape all in one breath. From that moment, whenever anything mechanical went wrong, we turned to Peter. Owning sound equipment which would be more at home in a computer factory, he is a mechanical wizard.

For technical skill it would be hard to rival the town of Darrowby. 'They'll never do it,' I said as I looked at the busy main square of Richmond, Yorkshire, that would be turned into the quieter market town of the 'thirties.

Centering Skeldale House in the market square and using a beautiful house owned by the Turners for it, the rest of Darrowby was made up of a number of villages with Askrig the main one. The shots you see of the market square from inside the house are a big, specially-painted backdrop that runs around the outside of the studio 'house'. The most frequent example you hear explaining the fragmented nature of film work is of a man who walks up a street and into the door of a house. That happens one day, but it might be not until several months later the schedule allows him to complete his action and come into the hall on the other side. So it was with *All Creatures Great and Small*. It was all the exterior work we filmed around Yorkshire, the interiors were studio mock-ups.

Despite our misgivings, the market square *was* transformed. The sequence we filmed was when James Herriot first arrives in Darrowby. It was within the first few days of us starting to film around, and it was Carol's first day. The hotel in which we based the costume and make-up departments was late opening that morning. Needing to start at about eight a.m. to do the day's work, it wasn't until an hour later that we could get in. Adding to the nervousness Carol must have felt, the make-up department had to rush the job – not very reassuring for an actress whose character is introduced for the first time at the start of a long series. Those first few moments are important. You need to establish the character from the word go.

As the clock ticked by, the market square became filled with 1970s cars and 1970s people going about their business. The camera was angled so it would only film small sections at a time. They could be cleared and the prop-men would set to work covering road signs and advertising hoardings with hardboard and mud and carefully concealing yellow lines from view.

One of the benefits of the decline in British Cinema is the excellent people who now work in television. Our cameramen were Ken Morgan and John Kenway. Their contribution to the series is enormous, the shots of Yorkshire stunning by any standards. The only catch is that there are so many first-rate cameramen working in television that the photography you think should win an award for its brilliance is equally good in the next programme you turn to. Judges at award-givings must have a very difficult time of it! However well an actor might get on with the director, it is the cameraman who is actually filming him. It is his advice on what movement or facial expression looks good through the camera that makes all the difference to how your performance comes over on television. An actor, knowing this, always checks with the cameraman that an action is all right with him. A bit nervous and hesitant as we were at the start of filming, and trying hard to give our performances the right humorous quality, it was three days before Ken and John actually smiled at our antics. We were becoming a bit desperate by then, wondering what the devil was wrong. Once they had thawed towards us they would constantly give helpful and constructive advice.

Drawn up in the car park as we started the filming was Siegfried's car. Wedged in beside a lot of modern cars, it looked just like one of a row. A young police constable inspected the cars as he went through the square. Occasionally he would write out a parking ticket and slap it on a windscreen. When he came to Siegfried's he couldn't believe his luck. There, set in the windscreen, was a tax disc that was not just out of date, but out of date by forty years. His parking tickets snatched from his pocket, his pen flew across the page in glee. At that moment his superior officer who was over to check we were all right came up and explained to him. He must have been crestfallen, his visions of rapid promotion dashed.

chapter seven

I was enjoying things. *All Creatures Great and Small* was ticking along well. We were relaxing and, though sometimes hard-pushed to keep up the schedule, we were all getting on. I discovered I really enjoyed working with the animals. I took pride in the small amount of skill in handling them I had acquired. If a job looked difficult to do then I liked it the more. So frequent were my dips in and out of cows' rear quarters that within a short time we were all very blasé about the whole thing. 'Here we go again!' the camera-crew would groan as, to the cries of 'Chris is at it again' from the rest of the unit, I rolled up my sleeves. Robert Hardy always managed to avoid it. 'Here, you do it James,' Siegfried would say at the last minute, but Peter Davison was soon a dab hand.

The extraordinary thing about it was, in the way you see in cartoons, the cows would turn around, hay hanging from their mouths and, giving you a cursory inspection as your hand plunged in deep, tip you a wink. I know they have a habit of blinking with only one eye, but sometimes the timing was uncanny.

A very satisfactory moment came when we were doing a sequence of Herriot cleaning a horse's teeth. The horse we used was a great big cart-horse. As I rehearsed the shot, rasping away with a large file-like object at its teeth whilst firmly holding its tongue, the farmer whose animal it actually was leaned back against the barn door idly watching.

'So when's the actor going to come then?' he asked.

'I am the actor,' I replied.

'Don't be daft,' he said. 'When's this guy who's playing Herriot goin' to come?'

'It's me,' I insisted. 'I play the vet.'

Maybe it was the way I looked, for he didn't believe me until the camera started rolling.

We did two 'takes'. The second time the cart-horse, who had been gently snuffling in my ear, carefully placed his tongue into my hand for me to hold.

Down at Farnham for *Taming of the Shrew*, for an entrance I rode on to the stage on a horse. Quite spectacular to have a horse in a 'live' theatre, even more so when you consider what a tiny stage the Farnham Theatre has. This horse was an evil creature. No one could go near it without it flailing the air with its teeth and legs. For some reason I was the only one it didn't object to. Perhaps it knew I was about to play a vet and it was advisable to stay in with me.

There was a scene in *All Creatures* when we needed to have a bad-tempered, snappy little dog. For that episode we had Ken Ives directing us; at one time an actor and famous for 'Hawk-Eye', he was now turned television director. As he walked through Richmond to join the film unit, he passed a parked car. In it he could see a small dog beadily watching him. As he approached the animal went berserk, snarling and snapping through the windows. He discovered the dog belonged to a woman who readily agreed to bring it down to the studios in Birmingham when the time required. Arriving at the studios, for some reason the dog decided it liked me. Quite happy to snarl at everybody else, it would give me a lick as if to say, 'Don't worry, mate. I'll soon get this lot sorted out!' and set about anyone who came near us. Even after I had been shown how to make it snarl at me by pinching its stomach, contrary to everything in the script, we still remained the best of friends. It obviously hadn't read its contract properly. It was not prepared to perform, so we had to fudge it. Filming my face, we used a recording of him snarling and made it look as it should have done in the first place.

If I was priding myself on an affinity with animals, it was creatures like Boris the cat who sharply reminded me of my place.

Boris was recreated using a very large, tetchy ex-tom. The scene was supposed to run in the following way. Boris, a wild-looking animal, was to leap from his basket. Catching him, I was to wrap him in a towel and put a pill down his throat. His 'owner' was to stand in front of me looking on. In the way cats do, having protested heavily at being placed in his basket, when the moment came for him to leap out he decided he really rather liked it and was quite happy to spend the next few days in there. He was not to be persuaded. With a glove puppet which when filmed at the correct angle would look as if it was Boris, Mike Treen, the production assistant, dodged down out of camera-shot and made the puppet look as though it was Boris leaping. As time was getting on we decided to settle for that.

I picked up the real Boris and wrapped a towel around him. He didn't like that at all. His eyes flashed and his tail beat the air, but I had him firmly held to me. With my free hand I went to put the pill in his mouth. During rehearsals I had worn a pair of gauntlets, but they had been too cumbersome and so I decided against them. But Boris had had enough. His razor-sharp teeth closed tight over my finger. His fangs must have met in the middle. With a scream of indescribable pain, I dropped Boris. He clawed his way up the skirt of the 'owner' who stood opposite me, over her shoulders and down her back, from there making good his escape. Professional in the extreme, the actress said nothing, at most letting out a gasp from between clenched teeth. Later in the make-up room she took off her blouse. Boris had left a precise track of deep lacerations over her. They must have taken weeks to heal. Unfortunately, but quite naturally, as Boris's teeth sank in it was an obscenity I had yelled. Boris, having made his objection quite clear, was sitting smugly washing himself just a few feet away. None of us was prepared to do the scene again. Perhaps it makes for better television the way it turned out. The sound boys were able to erase my screams and it was shown the way it happened: too painfully real!

All forms of swearing were of course strictly disallowed. The programme was to go out on Sunday evenings directly after the religious hour. We regular characters weren't even allowed to refer to a 'cow's arse', as all the rural characters were. In the cricket match sequence Mrs Pumphrey's chauffeur said to James

Herriot, 'Bet you've never removed a cricket ball from a cow's arse, vet!' But what I always felt to be most unfair was they were even allowed to say 'bugger', not once but over and over again. We regulars would try to sneak the odd swear word into the script. After all, sometimes it was much more natural to curse. We would giggle to ourselves during rehearsal and when it came to the appropriate moment we would drop our voices so no one could quite hear. Reading their scripts, the production team would, we hoped, automatically assume we had said what was in the script. Just as we would be nudging each other at our success the script editor, who missed nothing, would come over and dryly say, 'I think we'd better stick to the words as they are written in the script, don't you?'

Only once did I ever manage to swear. There was a scene where Tristan had been sick in my car. Of course he was hopelessly drunk.

'You've been sick all over the passenger seat,' James Herriot yelled at the semi-conscious Tristan.

'Have I?' he asked blearily.

'Yes you bloody well have!' Herriot snapped,

Not very strong, but I made it.

Some while later, when being interviewed on a television chat show, I was asked what I thought made the series so successful. Remembering an article I had read analysing the programme, I answered glibly, 'No sex, no violence, no bad language.' This was true, but there was a lot more to it than that. Perhaps I was asking for the letter I received from an irate viewer. 'Dear Mr Timothy,' it began, 'when will you get it into your head that sex, violence and bad language does not necessarily constitute a bad programme.' Quite right. But not when it came to *All Creatures Great and Small*.

There are a number of sequences involving characters getting drunk. Only the briefest glance at an episode is needed to see clearly drink is not a good thing. Often the joke is on Herriot as he is made to stumble about, a naïve victim of someone else's vice. Imagine then how stunned I was when, giving another interview, the first question I was asked was how did I feel about the furore in the Scottish press and television that blamed the programme as having an irresponsible and thoughtless influence on drinking patterns? I was the more upset because the implication was that I, Christopher Timothy, was personally responsible for the rise in alcoholism.

If only those people in the media had known the true facts behind the scene to which I think they most objected.

James Herriot has taken a dog over to another vet known for his rumbustious and high-living ways. Unlike the Farnon–Herriot practice, which is a bit short of money, this other vet is well-to-do and has a surgery equipped with all the latest gadgetry. After operating on the dog, the vet insists Herriot come with him to the pub for a drink or two. This vet, incidentally, was wonderfully played by James Grout, who featured in a number of episodes. At the time of writing this book Jimmy sent me a card from Epping Hospital. Going to visit him I found his legs in traction. He would be strapped up in bed that way for two months, he told me. Out riding, his horse bolted. Nearing a main road, Jimmy had realized there was nothing for it but to jump. He had severely fractured a leg.

Anyway, this vet Jimmy Grout played drags the reluctant Herriot into the pub and slaps down three pints of beer in front of him. For some reason I have never liked the taste of beer. The props department had assured me they were trick glasses; a pint mug has a transparent cylinder running down the middle. When filled it looks as if the half-pint it contains is in fact a whole one. The 'beer' we had was very flat shandy with an alcohol content of about one per cent.

As we sat there playing the scene I downed the first trick pint. It was fairly horrible to do but I could keep this up, I reassured myself, as I reached for the second pint. To my horror I saw the second pint was not a trick one, but was filled to the brim with flat shandy. 'Goodness. Here goes,' I thought to myself as I carried on acting. Halfway through, the other vet says, 'You've still got another one left,' and points to the third. To my relief the third one was a trick glass. Although feeling distinctly odd by this time I kept going with the scene. Having got through it we left the pub. As we got to the door and it swung shut behind us the cameras stopped recording and the scene ended. Instantly I threw up all over the place. At that moment the director said over the tannoy which linked him from the control gallery to the studio floor, 'OK. Let's do that scene again.' From where he was he couldn't see us, concealed as we were by a piece of scenery. The make-up girl quickly dabbed my face and we started the scene over again. I got through the first 'pint'. I was halfway through the second, this time another trick glass, when Jimmy Grout, as the vet, said his line, 'You've still got another one left.' As he pointed, unable to help myself, I threw up again, but this time all over him.

At the National Theatre I remember being late for rehearsals and haring in at the stage door. Rounding a corner at the speed of light I bumped straight into Noël Coward, someone without whom any theatrical memoir would be incomplete. 'I'm awfully sorry,' I said, appalled.

'No, no. The pleasure was entirely mine,' he replied debonairly, gathering himself together. It reminds me to be wary, not only of going round corners, but that people can interpret your actions in quite another way to the one you meant. I suppose the motto is 'Carry on regardless'; old actors, dismissing the complex theories of modern drama as tosh, say, 'Speak loudly and clearly and don't go knocking into the furniture.' A school of thought experience shows it wise to believe in.

Another time something I said in an interview was twisted to mean something quite different. Again it was a television chat show. 'Do you like animals?' I was asked. After a moment's thought I said decisively, 'No.' The studio audience fell about with laughter. I meant of course, and I think in its proper context it was quite clear, I like animals but I wasn't prepared to go barmy about them in the way some people do. They seem to care more about animals than people. When I said this one evening at dinner Jack Watkinson agreed with me. He said that if the Royal Society for the Prevention of Cruelty to Children made an appeal, for every £1,000 they received, the Royal Society for the Prevention of Cruelty to Animals would be sent £10,000. Illogical in the extreme. Jack told me that most vets would feel the same way; children first, animals second. But the *Sun* ran a banner headline: ' "I don't like animals," says TV's vet.'

My two youngest children are black. 'Do you think it a good idea for a black child to go to a white family?' asked the man at the adoption society when Sue and I applied for David. We had already adopted Kate some two years before. Having considered it all very carefully for many months, there had never been any doubt in our minds that, firstly, chances were it would be a black child anyway and, secondly, that the child being black would cause no problems. I was able to say quite firmly to the man, 'Yes. I do think it a good idea.' Our family had accepted Kate quite naturally, and we all love her very much. Having brought her back to the house, we gathered around. The kids having satisfied themselves that the colour wouldn't rub off, Sue and I explained to them her parentage was West Indian. Clutching her to him, Nicky said, 'But if she's West Indian she'll grow up not understanding a word we say.'

Near to us in Surrey is a large school that in holiday time opens its gymnasiun to the local kids. Supervised by the games master, the star attraction is the trampoline. My two eldest kids have keenly attended every session. Driving over to collect them one day, Sue had Kate with her who was then about three years old. The supervisor asked if any children who had come with their parents would like to have a go. Kate and Sue joined the queue. Next to them stood another little girl with her mother. The little girl was probably about five. She was transfixed by Kate and stared and stared. Finally, unable to restrain herself any longer, the little girl asked, 'May I touch her?' Kate giggled as she did so.

'How old is she?' she asked as she drew back her hand. Sue answered that Kate was three.

The little girl was silent, her eyes rounder than ever. After a moment she looked up at Sue again. Earnestly she said, 'I wasn't black when I was three.'

In my experience no child is racially prejudiced unless he picks up the attitudes of grown-ups. I try hard not to influence my kids in any way with what I feel to be my own life-hardened attitudes. They must be free to make their own decisions and be honest in the decisions they make. Certainly colour prejudice is something they have no time for.

A couple of years ago, taking Kate, Tabitha and the dog, we went to have a stroll round the village fête. One of the organizers, a lady of local distinction, came over to say hello.

'Is this Kate?' she asked brightly. 'Isn't she beautiful! What a pity they ever have to grow up.'

I'm sure she meant it quite harmlessly, but if she'd thought about it she never would have said anything so horrible in its implications. Maybe I'm just touchy, but then it's exceedingly difficult not to be. I'm not as good as I should be at explaining, so when Tabitha asked, 'What did that woman mean?' I wished that Sue had been with me to help.

Sue is wonderful. Endlessly patient, she manages to say exactly the right thing. With a large family in tow it is a much-needed ability. Having a bath one day with a very young Simon she noticed he was staring between her legs in great consternation. He then looked down between his own legs. 'You haven't got a willy,' he said, horror-struck as he looked back at her. 'Here goes,' Sue thought as she lay back ready to give a long explanation. Before she could start Simon clambered from the bath. 'Don't worry,' he said, 'I'll go and get daddy's.'

People say you must be wonderful to adopt, but I think it is fostering that is remarkable. My brother Jon having been adopted, my mother later fostered a baby girl. We all fell in love with her. It was terrible when she had to leave.

Mum always kept in contact with Jon's natural mother. When he was about thirteen he asked Mum if he could meet her. Very nervously, I should think, Mum invited her over for the weekend. I don't know what we were all expecting, but it was the shock of our lives when up the path walked a nun. Mum must have been very brave to have organized the weekend from the start. Pre-occupied as I was with my own adolescent world of girlfriends and rock 'n roll, I was not much help. The nun bubbled and joked away, easing a lot of the tension. She was a wonderful woman who belonged to a secular order. I know it is not true, but I can't help thinking of nuns as a bit rarefied. A teacher, she was very down-to-earth in her approach. She spent the time with Jon going for long walks, the two of them alone. Left at home, Mum must have been very on edge. Coming back on Sunday evening having been out for most of the weekend, as I crept up the stairs careful not to disarrange the quiff that balanced Presley-like on the top of my head, my movement restricted by the tightness of my drainpipes, I heard Jon and Mum in the kitchen. Jon was saying, 'I like her very much, but she's more like an auntie. You're my real mum.'

Jon and his natural mother have since kept in contact. Later she left the order, not taking her final vows. Never in any way interfering with the life that had adopted him, she is, as Jon said, 'like an aunt'.

More than anything else in *All Creatures Great and Small* it is Tristan smoking that brings back the hit-or-miss days of my youth.

Peter Davison is a non-smoker but the character requires that he does smoke. Unable to have a cigarette with a filter, as it is the 1930s, he is provided with a packet of Woodbines – the most evocative brand of all! As a kid my mates and I would sneak under the railway bridge and pass round a packet that must have lasted us a fortnight. It was the image and not the nicotine we were after. It was so adult. A very definite part of the routine was to spit after every drag in imitation of the grown-ups. How I longed to have spots too. That was the ultimate in sophistica-tion. Within a couple of years my wish was more than granted. The bane of my life for the next ten years, the acne with which I broke out heavily conflicted with any romantic notions I might have had. The terrible thing was that with every spot I developed, my romantic streak became stronger. It was difficult to forgive Danny Kaye for kissing Virginia Mayo. Esther Williams just made life hell. Yet it was the cinema in Shrewsbury that became the focus of social life. The brash neon light of the foyer made all too apparent the drawbacks of adolescence. The light threw my acne into harsh relief. My face must have looked like Krakatoa. Examining myself in the mirror with the greatest care I would decide on which side of the girl I was hoping to impress I should sit. My profile also gave me cause for concern. Each night for several months I stuck sticking-plaster over my nose to help restrain its ever growing proportions. I had read in a magazine that this would help. It might have, but it did nothing for the spots which flourished underneath as though it was a dream come true. Drenched in antiseptic, I gave off a smell no hospital could compete with. I was soon identified as 'TCP Tim'.

One holiday I worked in a bakery. We were there at five-thirty each morning to mop the floors and ice the cakes. There was a girl whose birthday it was. Flush with the £2.10s I was earning a week, I offered to buy her a present. 'You can give me a pair of stockings if you like,' she said, 'but you've got to put them on me.' There was a definite gap between desire and reality. It was all I could do to prevent myself running out of the door in terror.

As I sat with a friend in the cinema trying to impress a couple of girls who were nearby, we mocked and jeered at the screen with all the studied coolness our sixteen years could muster. A bloke in the seat in front turned round and waved a flickknife at us. 'If you don't shut up I'll do you!' he said. It was Reilly, the scourge of Shrewsbury. Rumour had it he'd been in trouble with the police for violence. We sank down in our seats, the girls forgotten, and hardly dared to breathe for the rest of the film. With visions of our guts smeared from one end of the high street to the other, as the credits flicked up on to the screen, we tore from the cinema. We had a strong suspicion that Reilly's threat had not been idle. A year later I read in the papers that he had been hanged for murder.

It was at the grammar school that I really came into my own. Our uniform included a cap. 'To be worn at all times' was a strictly upheld regulation. I would not wear it and was caught capless on four successive Saturdays. The first three merely resulted in detention, but the fourth called for a special prefectorial meeting. 'What on earth do we do with Timothy?' they pondered. Eventually I was summoned. 'This is our decision,' the head boy, one year older than me, pompously pronounced. 'For one week you will have your cap tied on with binder twine.'

'Can't I use a tartan ribbon instead?' I asked facetiously.

'No!' came the categorical reply.

I got my own back by sticking daisies behind my ears. Pushing back the peak, I wrote 'Kiss me quick' across it. The attention I got was phenomenal. They would gather in groups to gawp open-mouthed. This was definitely not what the prefects had in mind. I was sentenced to stand throughout a lunch-break on a table placed on the stage of the assembly hall. The school was encouraged to come and jeer me. It was a glorious moment that turned sour. The whole thing had struck me as ridiculous in the first place. But if it was difficult to cap my head, it was now harder still to cap my notoriety.

For *All Creatures Great and Small* I was provided with a trilby and a three-piece suit. Of course it was different, being a question of characterization, but this too led to a few skirmishes with the costume department. The waistcoat was far too stuffy and formal for James Herriot, I felt. Also, Herriot would never have worn a hat, however 'period' it might be. I knew he hated the things. Again there was ill-feeling. I was insistent. The costume department yielded. They never thought to resort to binder-twine even though I knew where the daisies grew.

Peter Davison's costume of baggy trousers, fair-isle sweaters and short hair coincided with the fashion then being promoted. He looked the height of modernity in his costume. Carol Drinkwater was simply made for clothes.

There was a scene in the first series where Helen has on a white surgery coat. As she talks to James she takes it off. Nothing difficult about that, very routine. It was the sexiest thing I've ever seen. Both the director and I were unable to tell Carol that this was how this very ordinary gesture was coming over; after all, she was just doing what the script said. On the pretext of a 'technical hitch', hoping to avoid by constant repetition any hint of sexiness, the director made her do it over and over again. If someone has sex-appeal there is very little that can be done about it. Judging from Carol's fan-mail she definitely has. The scene remained spellbinding for quite the wrong reasons – not at all suited to seven-thirty on a Sunday evening! In the end the scene had to be filmed with the camera pointing in another direction.

If the animals could be a hazard, so too were those white coats that hung neatly behind the surgery door. The problem was there were several of them, and all different sizes. In rehearsal you would single out the one you would need to put on as the scene progressed. Nothing was that straightforward. Perhaps the props department would decide fresher-looking ones were in order and whisk them away before the scene was filmed, replacing them with others. Maybe, in the heat of the moment, the coat would become indistinguishable from the others as it hung there, its folds merging in with the next. In the event the enjoyment of many a scene from the actor's point of view was completely ruined. Always we would end up with a coat which either swamped us and whose arms swung about our ankles, or we would find ourselves struggling into something not unlike a strait-jacket. At the same time we would probably be holding down some animal which had chosen that moment not to participate. The craft of acting would be severely put to the test.

When things became fraught there was always Peter Davison's packet of Woodbines to turn to. Smoking, unless called for by the script, is strictly prohibited in the studio. Although I too am now a non-smoker, in the past it was a great relief to know there was someone with a ready supply, and around whom the smell of cigarette smoke was quite permissible.

Try as I might I couldn't give up smoking. When I was doing the film in Ireland, after three months I thought it would never end and allow me to go to Singapore to do *The Virgin Soldiers*, a film I desperately wanted to do. On the last possible day a large black limousine rolled into the field where we were working. Out got three of the production team, smartly dressed in suits and carrying briefcases. 'If they've come to say I can go then I promise I'll give up smoking,' I vowed to some unspecified deity for the thousandth time in my life. Having spoken to the director, they returned to the car. I was on tenterhooks and smoked more cigarettes than ever. No one said a word to me. During lunch-break I passed the director back and forth on the slightest of pretexts, hoping for some indication from him. I said 'hello' so many times he must have thought I'd gone off my head. 'Hello, Chris,' he would politely reply each time. For the past month I had spent my Sundays hitch-hiking to Shannon to have the inoculations I would need for the Far East. My arms were like puff-balls. Whenever it looked like I might have to give up hope of ever getting away on time, Michael York would remind me of how important it was. That day we were doing a scene involving 600 extras and goodness knows how many horses. All I had left to do then was my death scene. After lunch the director announced over the loud speaker, 'Right, everyone can go home except for . . .' and he looked at the piece of paper in his hand. 'Yes yes?' I wanted to shout. '. . . Christopher Timothy, two extras and a horse.' The field was cleared and I lay down with the two extras standing beside me. Having no blood capsules to burst in my mouth, they gave me a bottle. I took a swig. The director called 'Action!' the horse jumped over me, the extras looked sad, I spat out the blood, gasped and died. 'Cut!' yelled the director. 'Thank you Chris,' he said, but I was already away. Throwing off my costume as I went, I ran over the fields to the car that waited to whisk me to the airport. I'm afraid though it wasn't until the combined company of *All Creatures* set to work on me that I was able to give up smoking.

*

The propmen on *All Creatures* were astonishingly versatile, producing from thin air the very object it had only just crossed your mind to think you might want. Once we needed an old stone road sign marked with a fictional town. The cardboard and polystyrene we prepared didn't look right. Within half an hour the real thing had been hewn from a block of stone and set by the roadside. We were in the middle of the country. Goodness knows where the skill had suddenly come from, let alone the appropriate stone.

I was well prepared for all eventualities. If the film in Ireland had been a disaster then it had certainly taught me a lot. The massive swords with which we had been provided were made from fibre-glass; all, that is, except for mine. It must have been the real thing, dug from some peat bog. So heavy was it that with one swing I would be yanked the length of the field. None of this was helped by the fencing lessons we had been given. The Fight Arranger had got it wrong and had taught us to thrust and parry in a style that didn't develop until several hundred years later, and then it was with a sword the size of a knitting-needle.

We had come to do a battle sequence involving hundreds of extras. We heroes were waving our swords about and all around us the enemy were dropping like flies. I stuck my sword into the extra that faced me. Simulated, it looked like the real thing. The sword neatly plunged between his chest and arm.

'Die,' I whispered.

'No,' he said.

'Die! The camera's filming us!' I hissed.

'Oh,' he said and promptly fell down dead.

A fellow actor had broken his leg. In white plaster from the knee down, the camera only filmed him from the waist up. 'Be better if you painted the plaster red,' he joked to a prop-man. The scene progressed. A few minutes later, out of the corner of our eyes we saw the prop-man crawling under the table towards us. From his mouth dangled a pot of red paint and a paint brush.

Broken legs! A recurring theme. I should have been warned it was only a matter of time before something happened to me.

Only two weeks into the filming of *All Creatures* came the first horrible reminder.

Although the animals used in the filming were quite often found by Jack Watkinson, it was the production assistants who mostly searched out what was required. Bill Harmon was our first. A cockney lad with interests in the music business, I don't think he'd even seen a cow close to before the series began. He was phenomenal. The farmers spoke highly of him. He often found animals who only the week before had had the illness required by the script. It was purely coincidental. The farmers would stand out of shot sagely nodding their heads. Provided with a Land Rover, he worked round the clock. Late one night whilst driving over the moors, his Land Rover broke down. Standing on the bumper with a torch he leaned over the engine examining it. At that moment a car came hurtling round a bend. It smashed into the front, crushing Bill's legs. Very severely injured, had he been standing on the ground he would have been killed outright.

His place was taken by Laurence. As with Bill, being a cockney lad, Laurence seemed at first totally out of place. He appeared quite other worldly, and had the serenity of a monk. But his enthusiasm was vast and, as with Bill, his contribution to the series enormous.

As we all became more knowledgeable about the animals, everybody felt free to chip in. Even the make-up girls, downing their powder and puffs, would have some constructive advice. Making the series everyone went over and above the call of duty. Often it was not just human faces the make-up department were concerned with. There was the kitten that had a sudden attack of nerves in the studio, requiring a make-up girl to follow it round with a mop and a bucket of water; the scene where Chris Brown as the uppity young vet Richard Comody falls into a midden and gets covered from head to food in pig manure; there was the sequence where I too, naked from the waist up, was plastered in cow dung. It was a cold night. I stood shivering as a make-up girl showed the director the simulated cow-dung she had made up from creams and colourants. 'No, no,' said the director, 'much better to use the real stuff.' He was only joking, I thought, as he took the jar from her and started to smear it over my chest. She slopped away covering my back. As it dried out, colder than ever I moved into position before the camera. Although the front of me felt fine, my back seemed to be developing the texture of leather. Within moments my skin became rigid as if encased in concrete. A quick scrape with my fingernails and the horrid truth dawned on me. The make-up girl had taken the director at his word. There I was, with every possibility of being famous, sitting in a cow byre at ten-thirty on an ice-cold night covered in shit. Forget the première and the glittering parties! This is what life as an actor is really like.

The farmer invited me into his house to clean up. I didn't dare go further than the kitchen. Standing in my underpants, the family set to with scrubbing brushes. More used to dirt than we were, every farm we worked on was as hospitable. Always we were invited to use the houses as our own. The general consensus of opinion seemed to be, 'By heck, it takes you back.'

chapter eight

At drama school, much to my amazement, I had won the Laurence Olivier Award for the best character performance. The skill they thought I had was tested to the full in episode eight of *All Creatures Great and Small*. For me it became known as my Sydney Harry Fox time. To look at the script now is to see something as stitched together as my body. Neither is dissimilar to a patchwork quilt.

Sydney Harry Fox was one of the portraits of a murderer in the Thames Television series *Killers*.

'They want you to do the part because you look just like him,' said my agent. I examined the photograph.

'Good grief! Is that how people see me?' I exclaimed.

In the event the cost of the wig I wore was more than my fee for appearing under it. It took the make-up department a good two hours to achieve the resemblance. A very long time. After my accident the same dexterity and positive thought was called for to make me look my former self.

During the weekend between episodes, I had gone over to Kent to join some friends in a 'treasure hunt'. I was well behind on the clues I had to collect. A chicken feather was next on the itinerary. Driving down a lane, I passed a farm. I stopped. I suppose I must have got out of the car and gone into the farm. Knowing only the injuries I received in the next few minutes, the actual circumstances have been pieced together by witnesses. They were obliterated from my mind. I don't know if I got the feather or not. I stepped from the gates straight into a car doing about sixty mph.

My head smashed the windscreen. My collar bone was broken. The thigh-bone of my left leg was smashed to a hundred pieces and broken below the knee. My right leg was severely cut about. I was bruised and battered. The nerve muscles in my arms 'buzzed' for the next year, limiting the use of my hands. I fetched up flung like a rag doll a few feet in front of the car. Apparently I asked for a cigarette. One was held to my lips. I was told or I have some recollection of someone saying I mustn't smoke, of a voice replying, 'Let him. He's only got about ten minutes to live.' Rumour, I think! A newspaper reported I had a metal plate inserted in my skull. My brain was so damaged, work-mates were told, I would never be more than a living vegetable. Mis-reports abounded in those few days that followed. The ambulance men of course didn't let me smoke, for several hours I wasn't even allowed pain killers. My head injuries were such that until the extent of them was established all I could do was to lie there whimpering and screaming obscenities when anybody touched me. The mercy of it was that for the first week I was deeply concussed.

They had found the address of my brother Jon. He was the first to be informed. The hospital would not tell him more than that I was severely injured, even though he is a medic himself. Specializing in genes, he is a pre-natal diagnostic. His boss phoned through to the hospital for him and within twenty minutes came back with a report. Apparently it was a great stroke of luck, the Medway Hospital to which I had gone was the very best place I could have been taken for my injuries. With the surgeon, Mr Haye, I was in the best possible hands. I must say how right that was. I am deeply indebted for the treatment I was given, the wonderful way I was put back together again. This despite my intolerable behaviour to anyone who came near me. The nursing staff were remarkable and needed more than just the ability to be 'ministering angels'. They even brought me a television on which to see episodes of *All Creatures*. On reflection, I would have thrown it at me!

People ask why I didn't sue the driver of the car. She must have had more than her fair share of shock. I was just happy to be alive. Neither of us took action against the other.

We were in the middle of an important and expensive new series. The timing of the accident from everybody's point of view could not have been worse. The speed with which I was back at work, six weeks, the torture it was, has made me appear some kind of hero. That I definitely am not. For me, if the BBC had said to take six months off, it wouldn't have been long enough.

I was motivated by the terrible guilt I felt at messing everyone about, as well as a horrible fear that I would be dispensed with and a new James Herriot found. If in the ensuing months life was tough for me, unfortunately I know I made it hell for everyone else.

I spent a month flat on my back in hospital, and metal plates were put into my leg to re-create the thigh-bone. Extensive physiotherapy followed, given by a wonderful girl at the Charing Cross Hospital. One of the difficulties was that the time spent immobile had wasted away to nothing the useful bits of me that were left. Although physical difficulties were extreme, I'm told fifty per cent of it was psychological.

Added to this was the awful fact of my marriage breaking down. I was discharged and went home to Sue. Before we had married she had qualified as a nurse. Sue was wonderful, she knew exactly how to cope. But the accident put pressure on something where no pressure should have been. We both knew that, as fond as we were of each other, we had fallen out of love. The accident and my total reliance on her crippled the increasingly fragile bond between us. It magnified the problems and made them temporarily insurmountable. As much as we were willing to try, we no longer wanted to be together.

The cast and directors of *All Creatures* were magnificent. Returning to work so soon was the best therapy I could have had. Laden with pain-killers, I was barely able to walk, and then only with the aid of a couple of sticks. My fellow actors didn't know what to expect. What a lot they had to put up with. I was determined to be as near as possible to how I was before. I thought the first day back wasn't too bad. I was told later the rest of the cast just looked at each other and shook their heads.

I have written earlier of the technical wizardry required on the part of the directors. The production team had to create from the pile of rubble that was me a James Herriot who looked as though he could walk and run. During my six weeks off, the cast had worked round my absence as much as possible. They recorded sections of later episodes and, breaking the precisely planned timetable, zig-zagged about. Actions calling for difficult movements from Herriot had been given to the other characters. As I said, the script for episode eight looked like a patchwork quilt.

Viewers will have noticed conversations round the dining-room table to be an important part of every episode! The running together of scenes from a number of them meant that for those first couple of weeks back I seemed to be glued to the chair. All day meal would follow meal. I needing feeding up but this was ridiculous. I was going to be ill all over again!

The make-up department would fill the deep scar on my forehead with wax before I could go in front of the camera. A country bloom had to be painted on my haggard face. Youth had to be restored. It was truly Sydney Harry Fox time.

Problems! How to make it look as if I could walk in through the door when I couldn't put pressure on the more damaged of my legs? How could I do the simple action of walking into a room to talk to Tristan for example? It was resolved by the camera filming me pushing open the door, allowing me to remove the pressure by leaning on the handle. The camera would then cut to Peter Davison and hold while he pretended to watch me cross the room. Out of shot, I would frantically hop into position. When I was there, the camera would cut back as though it had all been quite normal. My antics must have looked very odd to Peter. As much as it hurt, we all laughed a lot.

Then too, how to descend a flight of stairs? Dressed in my costume, the feet of the production assistant were filmed pattering down. The camera cut. I quickly put on the costume and the camera filmed me standing at the bottom. Surely though, however much the script was altered, there was no getting round the scene requiring James to run across a field with a bucket. I should never have disbelieved. As shown the scene looked ace. The snail's-pace lollop I could just achieve was turned by the camera into something approaching the graceful movement of a young gazelle! It was magic. But I felt like Quasimodo incarnate,

A man from a well-known Sunday tabloid came to spend the day watching us at work in the studio. I had been told to rest when I could, to always sit in a wheelchair when the camera was not rolling, to use walking-sticks as much as possible. My dresser Bill was always there lurking a few feet away, ready to hand me the sticks or to push the chair on to the next set. Bill had to be more of a nursemaid than a dresser. It took considerable patience just to manipulate me into my costume and suffer my constant grumbling. I was anxious the journalist shouldn't be misled. I asked that he play down my physical difficulties, and if there was to be a photograph it should be an old one making me look fit and healthy. Out came the article: 'Christopher Timothy relying on pain-killing drugs makes his way from set to set, his body racked with pain.' But worse, the photo was of James and Helen sitting on their honeymoon bed. Carol looked blossoming, but I appeared to be about a hundred years old. The walking-sticks were plainly visible.

Our honeymoon bedroom had been completely rigged to allow me the utmost manoeuvrability. The joke was that whenever James and Helen were just about to relax, the landlady would come and bang on the door. James would have to leap up to answer it. Not being able to move made this decidedly difficult. The bed was pushed to within a couple of feet of the door. This enabled me to swing both on it and the bed. All I had to do was to throw my weight from one side to the other.

Returning to the studio drugged up to the eyeballs, in my dressing room I found bottles of brandy and scotch. The card with them was signed by the crew and read, 'Well done son, and now for some more palatable anaesthetic.' As I read the card there was a knock on the door. It was one of the animal handlers.

'Couple of autographs love,' she said sticking some photos under my nose. As I signed them she leaned against the doorpost, arms crossed.

'Don't like dogs much do you?' she said. Not so much a

question, more a condemnation. Thinking perhaps she had read the article ' "I don't like animals" says TV's vet' and goaded by her off-hand manner, I sharply replied, 'No.'

'Could tell by the way you handled them,' she retorted, took up the photos and left.

I was speechless. Such unpleasantness following so hard upon such kind goodwill. I needed the bottle of brandy to recover.

Watching the first few episodes I was only too aware of the most frequent criticism levelled at me. 'If he doesn't stop being so charming I'll put my boot into the television set,' a friend informed me of his views on watching. I had managed to ease up on that by the time of the accident. This was for the better. Ironic that the accident should have pushed it completely from my private life. At that time charm would have helped a lot.

Always hard-pushed and tired by everything, I was out on location filming a sequence with a colt. It was very frisky and nervous. The woman who owned it watched as I tried to control it. Helpfully she volunteered that if I continued to treat it in the way I was, it would kick me. 'Then I'll kick it back so hard,' I snapped, 'and I've got metal in my leg.' Goodness knows, had I been all right, then I never would have said anything as unpleasant. The forbearance and tolerance shown by everyone at all times was enormous. I only hope that, should I one day find myself in their position, then I will be the same.

chapter nine

'One boil and look at 'em!'

'No no no madam! You mustn't boil them,' exclaimed an exasperated Roy Newton, proprietor of Newton's Gents Outfitters, for the hundredth time as a Shrewsbury housewife pulled from her shopping basket a rumpled and yellowed rag.

'It were a new white shirt this. We was just thinking as to how we liked it.'

'But madam! It's a new fabric. Drip Dry it's called. You can't boil it. You wash it, hang it up and that's all. I told you when you bought it.' He pressed together his well-groomed hands in despair.

'Not as how I like to do me whites that.'

'I don't know, Siegfried,' James Herriot might have said had he been looking on.

As with Jack Watkinson, someone who very definitely did know was our studio consultant vet, Eddie Straiton. Along with Jack who was our location consultant vet, he was a stickler for authenticity. Unlike Jack he had worked frequently in television before. The author of a number of textbooks and an autobiography, he had had a regular programme giving veterinary advice. It was interesting to learn that he had also been in practice with the real James Herriot.

A continuous problem was what do vets do when they stand around in the surgery just talking? The most likely 'business', Eddie advised us, would be to grind powder in the pestle and mortar, to put pills into packets, or to label bottles. Undoubtedly the favourite was to pound with the pestle and mortar. I would rush into rehearsals only to find that Peter Davison had got there first and bagged it. Remarkable the abilities an actor suddenly develops in the cause of authenticity. Carol Drinkwater can hardly hold a paint-brush or sew in a straight line, yet there she is as the domesticated Helen Alderson doing both beautifully!

The scene where James takes a sick dog over to be operated on by the high-living well-to-do vet showed perfectly the extent to which Eddie Straiton was prepared to go in order that what we did on screen should be exactly right. The dog he found for us to use needed the same operation as did the dog in the story. We were always ready to improvise with a creature should it not behave in accordance with the script, making it look as it should. With this dog there was no need. The scene as it appeared on the screen showed James Grout and myself getting the dog ready, the camera then cut to Eddie Straiton's hands injecting the dog with anaesthetic. The scene that followed was a short one of the end of the operation. The two of us stood over the dog's prostrate body as it lay on the operating table and acted finishing off the operation and wiping up. When the scene, which had only taken a few moments to do, ended Eddie took the unconscious dog to the mobile surgery he had parked outside the studio. As we carried on recording the episode, Eddie operated.

Another time some people had brought a sick dog to him. He advised them the dog would need operating on. Told the cost of it would be some forty or fifty pounds, these people had instantly said no, it was too much. Callously saying, 'Put him down will you?' they had left. It was quite clear that the dog was beautifully tempered and once given the operation would have a good few years of active life in him. Equally, it was only too apparent that his owners didn't give a fig for him. Eddie operated and advertised for a new owner to whom, in exchange for the dog being provided with a good home, he would give free veterinary service for the rest of its life. We used the dog for an episode of *All Creatures*, as it had exactly the operation scar we needed.

Another problem with which we were repeatedly faced was how to open a scene in the surgery. It seemed too obvious if, as the scene began, an owner and animal merely came into the room and started talking. We felt it added depth if we could first show

114

the very end of the previous consultation. Doing that would imply to the viewer that 'surgery hours' had already been going on and that the visitor of this particular scene, although part of the storyline, was really just one of the many that came to see us.

It was great fun in rehearsal to make up these 'tag' lines. As a scene opened I would be giving an animal back to its owner saying something like, 'There you are, Mrs Truscott. Perhaps you would bring him in for me to see next week.' Mrs Truscott, played by an extra, would then cross out of the surgery as the next person, the real reason for the scene, came in. Inventing these lines must have released some of my frustration as a one-time author and director of amateur pantomime. This was all too clear on the occasion I decided I would be handing back a rabbit to a small boy. 'The reason it's not going to have babies is because it's a man rabbit,' I said and fell about with laughter. Everyone else just looked a bit pained.

It was pantomime that had provided me with my first link with our producer Bill Sellars. Whilst working on *Murder Most English* an unforeseen and tragic event had occurred. The series producer was Martin Lisemore. One of the most remarkable producers in television, he had to his credit successes like *I, Claudius* and *The Pallisers*. Above all, with easy nature and ready smile, he was greatly loved by everyone he came in contact with.

Just starting the second episode, we learnt that driving back to Oxfordshire he had been killed in a car crash. It was devastating news for all who knew him. Under such inauspicious circumstances Bill Sellars was called into take over from him. Just as effective as Martin Lisemore, Bill has a very different way with him. Where Martin was outgoing, Bill is quiet and reserved. Nobody could have wanted to take over from Martin and I'm afraid, stunned as we were, we were not very welcoming. For a time, Bill remained a distant figure with little contact between us. In that ubiquitous canteen in Birmingham he sat at a table by himself whilst a group of us were at another. None of us liked the idea of that and so we invited him to join us. It was breaking the ice time as we searched for topics of conversation.

I remembered hearing Bill had once played Dame in amateur pantomime and said so. The others looked a bit taken aback, but when it came to pantomime we both of us could have happily rattled on for hours.

I had written five of them for the Hatfield Heath Players, an amateur drama group I had co-founded several years before. The problems of paying royalties for performing an already published pantomime script for a group with no money could be got round by my writing a new one. It was great fun. For five years the Hatfield Heath Players had absorbed all my free time. Few things gave me such satisfaction as directing a production or putting together the set from bits and pieces donated by other enthusiasts.

Pantomimes have a strong morality underlying the innocent horseplay that makes them such fun as they bounce and rollick along. So does *All Creatures*. It is fresh and clean and has its values in the right place. It is comforting to the viewer to see that in this late-twentieth-century confusion there is a time and place where things do still have a happy ending. As with pantomime, one false move and the illusion is shattered, the thing turns sour. Bill Sellars kept a very watchful eye on the proceedings to ensure this wouldn't happen.

It was my unfortunate habit at the end of a scene involving an animal, as the cameras stopped filming, to pretend I was going to duff it up. 'Bash bash bash!' I would say as I mimed bringing down my hand on it. It was just an expression of high spirits and relief that the scene had worked. 'Tell Chris to stop that at once,' came the message, 'it gives quite the wrong impression.'

Again it was those tag lines. James was to open a scene by putting a canary back in its cage. 'There you are, Mrs Akroyd,' I was to say, having clipped the canary's claws. I was warned to be careful in the way I handled the bird. Too much heat from my hand would affect the canary's heart, killing it. With the bright lights the studio was warm so I was extremely cautious. 'There you are . . .' I said, placing the canary on its perch. Before I had finished the sentence it fell to the floor of the cage, its legs in the air. '. . . Mrs Akroyd,' I finished feebly. To our great relief, overcome by the excitement of it all, the canary had only fainted.

However much care we took in dealing with the animals, there were circumstances well beyond all our control. The saddest occasion was the making of the sequence where James delivers a calf.

We were all set to go. The pregnant cow stood in the byre, Jack Watkinson hovered attentive by the camera as it filmed. Everybody involved in *All Creatures* wanted to watch. Jack had tied a rope to the feet of the calf in the womb. I pulled on it with Jack pulling as well out of camera shot. Out came the calf. With a thud it hit the decks. I jumped on it as I had seen Jack do to scrape away the mucus from its nostrils and pounded on its chest to make the lungs work. An emotional moment. Everyone was transfixed. I was deeply stirred by responsibility for this new life. I rapidly worked away. But something was wrong. The calf remained motionless. Jack rushed over and as the camera stopped filming started to give the calf the kiss of life. For some minutes he desperately pumped away. We stood about watching, feeling helpless. No good. The calf was still-born. It couldn't have been a sadder anticlimax. Some of the girls turned away in tears. I felt it had been my fault. Examining the calf Jack told us it had probably been dead for at least two days. Still-birth amongst cattle, he said, was a frequent occurrence. It was just our misfortune. There was nothing any of us could have done.

On a more practical level, finding the right cow for the story, and setting up the cameras for the birth had taken a lot of time. The calf's death could ruin the tight schedule to which we needed to work. We returned despondently to our hotels and wondered how the story could be salvaged. Arriving on the set the next day, what seemed a minor miracle had happened. Another cow had just given birth. There in the byre lay a healthy calf that was an exact colour-match to the one the cameras had already filmed leaving the womb. Its timing into the world could not have been bettered. Seldom can a calf have been welcomed with such rousing enthusiasm from so many people.

The Yorkshire moors could be fiendishly cold. In the summer months, as people sweltered everywhere in the flimsiest of clothes, we would be filming up on the moors wrapped in every available garment we could lay our hands on. If the summers were bad, the winters were unbelievable. I now fully understand how desperate it can be when I hear on the weather reports that snow has fallen on the Yorkshire moors.

The wedding between James and Helen had been scheduled for summer filming. Because of some disorder, it had been postponed. One November day we stood around in our summer clothes and nearly shrivelled away with cold. For the men it was not so bad. Under our suits we could put on as many layers of Therma wear as would fit. Carol smiled and pretended it was the happiest day of Helen's life. Between her and the elements was nothing but the flimsiest piece of satin. What a tough time of it girls have. I always admire the stamina of the models you see in the papers showing next summer's swimwear. For some sadistic reason the photographers drag the girls to the nearest park. As they stand there all smiles and glamour, snowdrifts are clearly discernible in the background. A closer examination shows goose-pimples to be standing out all over their exposed flesh. We were kept going, goose-pimples and all, that November wedding day by a kindly extra who had a flask of hot coffee.

Location days were certainly enlivened not only by the fun we had as we acted out the stories and coped with the animals, but by the humour and high jinks that must necessarily arise when forty or so people work together. A lot of the things that happened had us in stitches, but were really only funny because of the situation at the time, the silly everyday things of people being together that are not worth repeating. If it could only be as simple as it was for one small boy who, with a serious expression on his face and apropos of nothing in particular, informed me, 'I get all my jokes from a book I got at London Airport.'

At one time a lot of us were staying at a certain hotel. I'd better not mention the name of it. We regulars were there for quite a long period. Visiting actors who came up for only a few days would find that, as crowded as the hotel was, indeed it had a room available and were given the key to Room One. This was a room to be avoided at all costs. Situated over the bar, the noise of the juke-box and the screams and shouts of the locals as they made merry would go on until four o'clock every morning. Not helpful if you had to get up at six. As the poor actor stumbled around bleary-eyed we would innocently ask, 'How did you sleep?'

Members of the technical crew were especially ingenious at arranging pranks. It was the episode of the cricket match. Urged by Helen who knows James can't play for toffee, and under the illusion that he is first-rate, the Vicar comes to beg James to be in the team. His mission accomplished, as the Vicar leaves the room, James mimes hitting the ball and then throws up his arms in triumph as if to acknowledge some vast crowd of spectators. As I put up my hands, a dodgy thing to do as I was still wobbly from my accident, loud peals of 'Match of the Day' music clanged out through the studio.

'Tristan's got a girl in here somewhere. I know he has,' says Siegfried, frantically rushing round the bedroom looking behind the curtains, under the bed and throwing open the doors of the wardrobe. Of course there is no girl for Siegfried to find. We did a dress rehearsal of the scene, and Robert Hardy tore round the room muttering the line. He looked under the bed, behind the curtains, he looked everywhere. He threw open the wardrobe and let out such a scream that we thought the studio roof would fall in. Standing there was a prop-man in full drag. Make-up was smeared across his stubbly face, a curly wig perched on the top of his balding head, and a great big smile stretched from one end of the wardrobe to the other.

If the characters were to spend such a lot of time sitting eating meals, then we hungry actors decided to make full use of it. Before going into the studio for the two days allotted to record each episode, instead of chancing our luck, we would order a menu. I have a passion for porridge and kippers. If it was a breakfast scene, this is what we got. Kippers became a joke, and the others would groan when, once again, kippers were placed before us. We thought it would give everyone a surprise if, as Siegfried, Helen, Tristan and James chatted away one breakfast, a kipper suddenly sat up and said, 'Rubbish!' Giggling away to each other we carefully tied a thread to one so that at the appropriate moment I could give the kipper a tweak. Carol would be its very high-pitched voice. Alas, we were scuppered. As the time approached, activity in the studio became frantic and it was inadvisable to have made any kind of joke. Sad, but I've never been able to look at a kipper in quite the same way.

One time when Robert Hardy had a heavy cold and was feeling so ill it was difficult for him to carry on, Eddie Straiton went to his bag and produced a very large pill. He didn't tell Robert what it was as he handed it to him and told him to take it, only that it would buck him up. It certainly did. If Robert had been running the Grand National on foot, he would have won by several lengths.

If Robert was feeling better, things were definitely out of sorts for Tricki Woo. It wasn't that Tricki Woo was playing the 'star' and wanted 'to be alone'; on the contrary, it was just a terrible breakdown in his relationship with other dogs. The story was that 'Uncle Herriot' had to bring Tricki Woo back to Skeldale House. On a less rarefied diet 'flop-bot' and 'cracker-dog' would be things of the past. Setting him down in the yard, the house dogs were to rush up and investigate. Tricki Woo, it would transpire, was in reality just a normal little dog. Making friends, they were all to do the doggy equivalent of marching off arm in arm into the sunset.

With Tricki Woo groomed up to the nines and very alluring, I set him down. What humiliation followed for Tricki Woo. The other dogs didn't want to know. He might have been no more than a bundle of rags. Nothing would persuade them that the requirements of the script must take precedence over their own feelings. It was clear, giving himself a desultory scratch, that Tricki Woo was going to develop an inferiority complex. What were we to do? Nervously, in hushed tones, we consulted together. Someone hit upon the idea of rubbing dog-meat behind Tricki Woo's ears. Mere common dogs as the others were, that surely would attract them. It was like sacrilege. You could tell Tricki Woo wasn't much taken with it, But he was a professional. Biting back the yaps of protest that any dog in his position might have made, he acquiesced. Humiliation followed humiliation. Not even that did the trick and the scene had to be abandoned.

Thinking of the two series of *All Creatures* we have made, of all the many things that might have gone wrong, there was not much that couldn't be salvaged. If a story required that a scene take place, with thought and dexterity on the part of the production team, it usually did.

James Herriot opens the door. There stands a little girl with a brown paper bag.

'Hello,' says James, 'do you want to see the vet?'

The little girl says nothing. James leads her into the surgery.

'What have you got in there?' asks James. Still the little girl says nothing. Taking the paper bag from her, James looks inside.

'Ah. It's a tortoise. What's his name?' The little girl remains mute.

'We'll call him Mr Tortoise then, shall we?' says James. Still the little girl says nothing. James examines the tortoise.

The scene ended with James putting it back in the bag and saying, 'Nothing wrong with him. But you bring him back whenever you want to.'

Reading the script, the scene appeared to be quite straightforward. Not even any potential trouble with the animal. After all it was hardly likely to attempt a ten-second dash for freedom. I would have liked my daughter Tabitha to have played the part. Robin had already made his debut as Edward III in the series *The Devil's Crown*. But at eight, Tabitha was a little too old for it.

We started filming the scene.

'Do you want to see the vet?' I asked. The little girl playing the part didn't say anything, but she shouldn't shake her head like that. I told her and we started again. It was all right, but this time the little girl didn't want to come in. I took her firmly by the hand.

'What have you got in there?' I said and pointed to the bag.

'It's a tortoise,' she said. The cameras stopped. I told her that she really wasn't supposed to say anything. We started that bit over again. 'It's a tortoise,' she insisted. Again the cameras stopped.

'You really mustn't speak,' I said, as gently as I could. There were tears.

'If you get it right I'll give you a sweet,' bribed her mother who was standing watching behind the camera. We decided to carry on. From now on, her mother told us, the little girl wouldn't say a word.

'What's his name?' I asked. My mouth was open and the words 'We'll call him Mr Tortoise then, shall we?' just forming, when the little girl said:

'Denis.'

'Oh! Fine,' I gulped. 'Then Denis it is.'

After that we didn't dare to attempt the scene again. Using what we had, the editor and the sound-men set to work. Deftly cutting the film and erasing the little girl's speech, the scene was reshaped into the one required by the script. I think, though, that even Harold Pinter and Shakespeare combined couldn't have found a more appropriate name.

Not only appropriate for the tortoise, 'Denis' seems to sum up all the fun and games we had with all the creatures, great and small.

At the time of writing, the making of the next series is two months away. If it was tomorrow, it wouldn't be soon enough.

James Herriot
All Creatures Great and Small £1.50
the first Herriot Omnibus Edition

Follow the career of the world's most famous vet from his arrival in the Dales countryside to the completion of his courtship of his wife-to-be, Helen. Meet the colourful Siegfried and Tristan and a host of unforgettable characters, both human and very much otherwise . . .

'Warm, joyous and often hilarious . . . there is humour everywhere' NEW YORK TIMES

All Things Bright and Beautiful £1.50
the second Herriot Omnibus Edition

This second omnibus takes up the story of the world's favourite vet from the closing chapters of *All Creatures Great and Small*. James is now married and living on the top floor of Skeldale House. He's a partner in the practice and his day is well-filled with the life of a country vet, bumping over the Dales in his little car en route to a host of patients from farm-horses to budgerigars . . .

'Absolutely irresistible . . . told with warmth, charm and never-flagging good humour' EVENING NEWS

All Things Wise and Wonderful £1.75
the third Herriot Omnibus Edition

The third Herriot omnibus takes up the story of the world's favourite vet at the outbreak of World War Two — swapping gumboots for goggles, he's transported from the Darrowby dales to an RAF training camp somewhere in England. Bashing the square or up in the air, he's daydreaming of the life — and the livestock — he left behind . . .

'Provokes a chuckle, or a lump in your throat, in every chapter' DAILY MIRROR

Daphne du Maurier
Myself When Young 95p
– the shaping of a writer

'A delightful book, full of amusing and charming stories, pinpointing the literary influences and the first stirrings of books to be written in later years, and with a happy and romantic ending' THE TIMES

'A world of famous names . . . Regent's Park and Hampstead . . . dinner parties, flirtations, grand winter holidays in Switzerland . . . Cornwall and the house by the river at Bodinnick' SUNDAY TIMES

Alan Burgess
The Small Woman 80p

The amazing true story of Gladys Aylward, the parlourmaid who became a missionary in China where, with great faith and indomitable courage, she worked for twenty years.

When the Japanese came to bomb, ravage and kill, she led a hundred homeless children on a terrible twelve-day march over the mountains to the Yellow River and safety.

Translated into many languages and filmed under the title of *The Inn of the Sixth Happiness*, the book is the inspiring record of the struggles and achievements of a most remarkable woman.

Daylight Must Come 75p

In 1953 Dr Helen Roseveare went out into the dark world of the Congo rain forests. She built her own hospital where she treated savage spear-wounds and lanced abscesses with iron-tipped arrows.

When the Congo erupted in revolt, Dr Roseveare stayed on – with only her faith and indomitable courage to protect her from pillage and slaughter, brutal beating and rape . . .

'A dramatic and poignant story of quite exceptional courage, human endurance and compassionate Christianity' THE TIMES

Eric Newby
A Short Walk in the Hindu Kush 60p

A wonderfully evocative account of a journey from Mayfair to the wilds of Nuristan.

'Eric Newby's depiction of their travels and travails is a total success' NEW YORKER

'A notable addition to the literature of unorthodox travel . . . tough, extrovert, humorous and immensely literate'
TIMES LITERARY SUPPLEMENT

'A pleasurable story of exotic and eccentric adventure'
NEW YORK HERALD TIMES

Patricia Jordan
District Nurse 70p

Born and bred in Belfast, trained in the hard school of student nursing, Patricia Jordan found her niche in a small Northern England town as a district nurse. With all the style of a born storyteller she tells of the patients and their case-histories — the comedy, tragedy and heart-warming humanity of her daily round — and of the doctors and nurses who work alongside her.

'First class . . . admirable reading' OBSERVER

Jay Anson
The Amityville Horror 80p

On 18 December 1975 George and Kathy Lutz, with their three children, moved into their new home at 112 Ocean Avenue, Amityville. Twenty-eight days later they fled from the house in terror . . .

'One of the most terrifying true cases ever of haunting and possession by demons . . . heart stopping . . . chilling'
SUNDAY EXPRESS

'The scariest true story I have read in years' LOS ANGELES TIMES

David Taylor
Zoovet 75p

The drowning hippopotamus and the arthritic giraffe ... The
pornographic parrot and the motorcycling chimp ... Just a few of
the patients that are all in a day's work for David Taylor, one of the
world's most unusual vets.

Zoovet is his story of the hilarity and the heartache of animal-
doctoring by jetliner across the globe.

'Good humour and abounding energy on every page'
WASHINGTON POST

Farley Mowat
The Snow Walker 75p

An unforgettable portrait of land and its people, capturing the
essence of the Arctic landscape and Eskimo lore.

'A vivid portrait of Eskimo life in the Arctic ... their fight for
survival in the harsh uncompromising environment'
MANCHESTER EVENING NEWS

'Stories of caribou, fox, walrus hunting ... hunger, famine, blinding
blizzard, of an Eskimo girl found in a snowhouse tomb ... of a
French lay brother's long trek with dogs to a remote tribe ... an
innate poetry' DAILY TELEGRAPH

Never Cry Wolf 75p

One man and a family of wolves in the northern wilds of Canada —
an all time clasic of animal lore ... The author, an acknowledged
expert on so many aspects of the North American wilderness, spent
one Arctic summer with a family of wolves, studying their daily
lives, admiring their loyalty and courage. This is the account of
those months, enlivened with warm humour and exploding the
vicious myths that surround the wolf, regarded by Mowat as 'a
highly evolved and attractive animal which is being harried into
extinction by the murderous enmity of man'.

'Splendid and satisfying. Wolves owe Mowat a debt of gratitude'
TORONTO GLOBE & MAIL

edited by A. L. Bacharach and J. R. Pearce
The Musical Companion £2.95

The classic musical reference book, first published in 1934 and a
steady bestseller ever since; now thoroughly revised and up-dated
for the world of music today: instruments of the orchestra – opera
– the human voice – chamber music – the solo instrument –
listening and performing. Contributors include David Atherton,
Eric Blom, Alan Blyth, Hugo Cole, Edward J. Dent, Robert Layton,
John McCabe, Charles Osborne, Francis Toye, and many more.

'The most useful, comprehensive and popular introduction to its
vast subject' DESMOND SHAWE-TAYLOR

Gail Duff
Country Wisdom £1

An encyclopaedia of recipes, remedies and traditional good sense.
The popular author of *Vegetarian Cookbook* and *Fresh all the Year*
has collected pages and pages of fascinating folklore, herbal
recipes, traditional advice culled from centuries of country life. Cures
for everything from insomnia to toothache, hints for home and
kitchen, traditional good sense and entertainment on every page.